WHEN MAMA'S HAPPY, EVERYONE'S HAPPY

WHEN MAMA'S HAPPY, EVERYONE'S HAPPY

THE MISSING HANDBOOK OF MOTHERHOOD

Regain your sanity, release guilt,
and restore your deliciousness

Allana Pratt
INTIMACY EXPERT

Copyright © 2020 by Allana Pratt

All rights reserved.

No part of this book may be reproduced in any form or by any electronic or mechanical means, including information storage and retrieval systems, without written permission from the author, except for the use of brief quotations in a book review.

To connect with Allana, visit allanapratt.com.

Contents

Introduction	vii
PART 1: THE BABE YOU WERE...	1
The Dirt	1
Single, Yummy Mommyhood	3
My Journey	5
Little White Mints	15
My Portal to Freedom	23
PART 2: THE BABE YOU ARE...	26
Addiction to Frustration	26
Momnesia: Who Am I Anyway?	30
Challenges That, Well, Challenge Me About Motherhood	33
Relax and Enjoy the Crisis	37
Struggle is Optional	39
PART 3: THE BABE YOU WILL BE...	43
It's Time to Teach	43
When Mama's Happy Basics	52
Powerful Practices for Sumptuous Motherhood	55
Eleven Hot Mama Solutions to Get Your Groove On	63
Life-Saving Practices for the Empowered Mother	70
I Just Don't Want to Have Sex!	79
Five Effective Tools That Strengthen Relationships	84

PART 4: THE BABE IS SINGLE?	90
No-Nonsense Dating Tips for Single Parents	90
Single Mom Perspective	92
Single Moms Creating Sparks of Passion	92
Guilt: This Single Mother's Middle Name	94
Mother's Day For the Single Mom	97
PART 5: THE BABE GETS THAT SHE'S A SACRED GODDESS...	101
We Never Get There So Go With the Flow	101
Seventeen Sexy Mom-Time Solutions With Your Little Muffins!	104
Nine Things to Stop Doing to Live With Strength, Sensuality, and Soul	109
THE Mother	113
Permission to Have It All	116
CONCLUSION: INSPIRING YOU TO LIVE LUSCIOUSLY FROM THE INSIDE OUT	119
Resources for You and Your Man	129
About Allana Pratt	131
Also by Allana Pratt	133

Introduction

Are you one of the millions of moms who yearn for more ME time, has lost your identity and passion for life, is feeling lonely in your marriage, or are you a single mom like me?

This happens so easily when we act on automatic pilot, trying to keep it together. I lose myself by being only in the role of mom, and I can't reconnect to my inner priestess, sultry siren or badass business diva, and then I struggle.

Sometimes when my son was younger, I couldn't see beyond the laundry to my true purpose on the planet. I felt so schleppy and out of touch with fashion that I didn't even want to try to dress well. I was running so fast, spinning from summer camp to the dry cleaners, that I forgot to connect, really breathe, slow down, open, and appreciate myself and the moment, so that I could surrender enough to FEEL the universe was on my side... allowing myself to be held, loved, and cherished like I truly wanted to be.

Familiar? Are you ready to change that? Are you ready to experience your luscious, juicy, radiance from the inside out, and to learn how to stay connected with your intuition and true feminine power? Do you feel ready to live your birthright, which is to be an empowered, confident, grounded, happy, glorious mom?

You'll find the magic pill on the inside back cover of this book... Ha! Gotcha! I wish.

No, there's no magic pill, yet there is a magic recipe.

It's worked for me, my clients, and community. And it will work for you.

Read these stories, follow these practices, and be open to small shifts and luscious miracles. Remind yourself you're filling up your tank first for your own inner happiness and joy, so you can share from the overflow with your family. Reconnect with your sensual nature for the juicy, luscious joy of loving being a woman. Then share that radiance with your partner, kids and the world by being YOU every day.

So luscious sister, make a commitment now to... Do your best with the practices.

Be kind, forgiving, and loving to your self.

Show up fully, even if you feel silly, angry, or sad. Remind yourself you're filling up your tank first for

YOUR own inner happiness and joy so you can share that with your family.

Reconnect with your sensual nature for the juicy, luscious joy of loving being a woman.

Share that radiance with your partner, and the world just by being YOU every day.

Let's begin.

While I understand how we yearn for the old days, how we want to get our sexy back, the fact is we can't go back. And nothing is more sad to me than someone in their 50's who keeps talking about the good ol' days in college, yet they missed savoring the beauty, richness and possibility of the past three decades, let alone the present moment. I don't believe we can go BACK in time to get our mojo. We're a new flavor of the feminine now, a deeper richer version, we're birthing a whole new delicious sacred YOU...

Sexy Sacred Mom:

> courageous woman who fiercely loves herself exactly as she is;
> tells the truth with bold kindness;
> is at peace in every inch of her own skin;
> her magnetic inner glow makes heads turn when she enters a room;
> gives herself permission to rejoice in her sexuality, and her body;
> gives the gift of her heartfelt self-expression;
> sees other sexy moms as sisters and celebrates them;
> knows asking for help makes life run smoothly;
> says "no" when she means "no," "yes" when she means "yes";
> speaks to herself with kind, compassionate, loving, sultry devotion;
> defines her true core wisdom as the Sacred Feminine, the Divine Mother; and,
> knows she's a juicy, luscious Goddess.

Sexy Sacred Mom is also known as Hot Mama, Yummy Mommy, Glorious Gift to the Planet.

Let's look even deeper at the word "sexy" and see if we can playfully restructure it a wee bit to empower us...

Sex-y: with a Y. *"Why don't you love me?"* *Needy.*
Sex-See: "See, I'm enough. And I love being a woman and mother."

I believe we are sex-see: sacred, succulent gifts to the planet.
I believe it is our birthright as women and mothers to be...

- The woman who turns heads when she walks in a room because she's at peace with who she is, and from the overflow, radiates joy.
- Confident with who she is, so full and flowing that she's always emptying herself out to be filled with passion, purpose, and spirit.
- So confident in her skin that she doesn't go through life comparing herself to others. She celebrates her sisters.
- So clear with her boundaries that she never gives from a place of obligation until she's depleted. Instead, she protects her precious energy and is able to give playfulness and patience to her family.
- So grounded and connected to the earthly plane that she breathes open from her womb to her eyelids, and attracts her husband magnetically.
- So authentic, kind, and real, and telling the truth without injury. This nourishes her soul regularly.
- A woman who knows she's enough in all her uniqueness and doesn't need to hide or show off, rather she can simply BE a gift to her friends and family moment to moment.
- A woman who loves being a woman: fiery love, luscious juiciness, deep sorrow, exquisite bliss, tranquil calm, like an ocean, at peace with all the changing tides.
- A woman who is balanced in giving to herself and to her family.
- A woman who receives support and encouragement, so that she may give fully to her relationships and career.

- A woman who loves being a woman: a creative powerhouse, sensitive to the slightest nuances, trusting of her instincts.
- A woman who is not ashamed to be off the mark, who realizes that mistakes are human, and so she inhales openly to each new moment, even if she's wobbly.
- A woman so fueled by the love for her kids that she's willing to show them a perfectly imperfect woman of authentic vulnerable grace, power, and joy.
- A woman so grateful to be adored, celebrated, and honored by her man, that she's juicy, radiant, and smiling on the inside just thinking of him.
- A woman so committed to being adored and cherished by her man that she'll always tell her truth with kindness and courage.
- A woman who is always open to doing the work for deeper connection and partnership; always open to getting her needs met.
- A woman who enjoys her ability to bring a man to his knees, yet never abuses her power, and shines her radiance as a gift of open-hearted love to the world.
- A woman who doesn't take herself too seriously, and who lets her child's youthful energy ignite her playfulness, dorkiness, and full self-expression.

Part 1:
The Babe You Were...

The Dirt

Pre-Gabriel my body was mine.

I knew it, I loved it, we worked. My time was mine. I could say "no," I had boundaries, I had time for me, and I was spontaneous!

My identity was mine. I was great at my job, I knew who I was, I knew what turned him on. I even felt turned on by me!

My life was mine. Then I became grumpy. Sleepless nights. No sex drive. No weekends off, ever.

Was I out of my mind?

All of this stirred up my "keep it together, look good, and feel in control" with life. It was as if every insecurity was churned up from the dark depths of my inner dungeon. I felt completely unprepared to be a mother, and I was insecure, questioning myself internally, yet I got fiercely defensive when I was questioned!

With the help of my coach, I discovered that my main insecurity seemed to have stemmed from an incident when I was about four-years-old, and had stolen The Flintstones vitamins from the cabinet and hidden with my sister in the closet to eat them all (because they were so yummy.)

My parents found out and told me I could have killed my sister. They were talking about taking us to the hospital to have our stomachs pumped. I was screaming in terror.

1. Because I was afraid for my sister's life, and
2. Because I needed them to know I wasn't evil!

They were so mad that I decided I *must* be inherently evil and could never trust myself again. I *must* be insane, I thought, because my good intentions had caused harm.

I've spent the rest of my life trying to be nice and stay one step ahead of everyone so as to cut off any chances of harming another.

I've paid the price of losing my authentic self-expression. It has cost me trusting myself as a woman and a mother, and disconnecting from my intuition. It has led me to believe the world is a scary place where I'm bound to hurt everyone eventually. It has cost me peace. It has cost me intimacy with myself and others, and with God. I'm beginning to laugh as I write this because I just couldn't face God and say I made a mistake with The Flintstones. What I think really did was make a mistake with me! (Yet I didn't want to hurt God's feelings either!)

The truth is this, illusion or belief has CREATED experiences for me to write about it all my life. I was stuck in trying to be the perfect mom until I let this one go.

The truth is I'm a good person. The truth is I can trust myself.

The truth is my intuition is very clear and I'm ready to birth the WHOLE me. The AUTHENTIC me, PEACEFUL,

CONFIDENT, DELICIOUS me, in a whole new way as a mother, lover, woman, and friend.

Thus it's time to write the missing handbook to motherhood, the one I wish I had, and the one I trust you'll enjoy.

Because it's basically a Universal Law that **When Mama's Happy, Everybody's Happy.**

WHAT THIS MEANS FOR YOU...

What do you have to forgive yourself for so that you can be happy, and peaceful?

Where do you need to put down the stick you're beating yourself up with?

Where do you need to wipe the slate clean, knowing you've ALWAYS done your best?

Where can you say THANK YOU to whoever pissed you off, hurt you, or betrayed you?

It's time to start fresh. Your kids and family deserve unconditional love and it starts with unconditionally loving YOU, beautiful.

Single, Yummy Mommyhood

So as most of you know, I got pregnant the week after my mom died.

At first, I thought I was mourning, then I blamed the hormones, then he convinced me I was sleep deprived.

No. No. And No.

It was the relationship.

As a single, motherless mom. The biggest lessons I learned were that being a martyr was really overrated, and that when I love and forgive myself, I can do anything.

Without child support or alimony, I had to face the truth

that hiding in the house, draining my savings, and using my son's tooth fairy money to go out for burgers wasn't going to cut it.

Single motherhood taught me that I couldn't run a kingdom unless I was a queen.

I asked for help. We moved into a tiny rental, and I learned about debt consolidation and generating cash flow.

While I hid at first, thinking I was only respected as a success if I could do it all on my own, I did begin to ask for help.

I went to church every Sunday, asked friends to babysit, and mentors for business guidance.

I learned boundaries like, "You can't come into Mommy's room until 'seven zero zero' because she's looking for patience and kindness." I learned to fill myself up with pleasure, friends, and yoga when my son was at his dad's, versus complaining as a lonely victim.

Gabriel and I focused on the good by blowing out candles after dinner making wishes for "painting with mommy" or "peace and miracles." We said "thank you's" every night at bedtime, expressing gratitude for our Mother Earth, strawberries, and even the bully because we learned to use our words, not our hands.

Being a single mom made me savor and cultivate morsels of joy. It gifted me with the courage and strength to surrender. It invited me to focus on what my ex-husband provided, rather than complain about what he didn't.

Most of all it made me leak what Gabe calls "happy tears"... being moved by the simple moments of extraordinary gratitude for being a mother.

WHAT THIS MEANS FOR YOU...

Where is your life the perfect laboratory for your greatest growth, and expansion?

How has every challenge perfectly molded, trained, and sculpted you into your best self?

What precious quality has been birthed in you because of your unique journey?

What strengths and super powers do you now exude because of your chosen path?

How can you love yourself MORE exactly as you are and exactly as you aren't?

MY JOURNEY

While the accent's basically gone, I am a small town Canadian girl who grew up loving guys with big trucks, Crispy Crunch chocolate bars, and walks in the woods. Who am I kidding? I still love guys in big trucks, chocolate, and walks in the woods. I was raised by a teacher mother and pharmacist father. While I enjoyed summers at the lake, most of my school years were spent feeling misunderstood for my expression, my enthusiasm, for feeling too much.

While my parents were divorcing, I looked to my grandmothers for encouragement and found the courage at nineteen years old to hop on my Uncle Phil's semi heading south to live my dream in Hollywood. While I was brave enough and talented enough—I sound like Stuart Small from Saturday Night Live... Ha!—I didn't have a work visa so the only job I could find was working in Japan.

I arrived there with forty dollars and lived in a cockroach-infested place I shared with fourteen other foreigners. Unwilling to turn back and have my family say, "I told you so," I became a successful model, dancer, and spokesperson on TV, magazine covers, runways, billboards, movies, and music videos. By year four, I was making more money than my parents combined. It was there I met my first husband: a tall, dark, and handsome multimillionaire. I followed him to NYC where we married. I graduated cum laude from Columbia University and worked for CNN, yet I was dying inside. While I loved him, in hindsight I don't really think I knew what love was and I was afraid to pass up a great guy and a picture-perfect life.

What if no one will ever love me again? What if no one this rich ever loves me again? (Embarrassing but true.)

As I felt this fear, I became a deeper, more sensual, and empowered woman. I was no longer a fit for the relationship and we divorced.

A few years later I had moved to LA, bought my own condo, was working as a life coach, and dating this argumentative, yet charismatic guy, when I found out my mom had cancer. She was sixty and had just retired. It all happened so fast. After an initial operation to "get it all," in ten days she was gone. The next weekend at my sister's wedding I got pregnant. Since I couldn't save my mom, I tried to save the relationship. This too quickly ended in divorce. I was a single, motherless mom and I hit rock bottom.

The journey to regain my confidence, self-trust, and self-love resulted in an unexpected by-product: sensuality. It was as if I'd attracted my niche as the "sexy mom expert" and walked into a seminar one weekend and met the (next) man of my dreams.

We were blessed to co-parent my amazing toddler, Gabriel, with my less annoying and ever charismatic ex-husband. I became a regular on Leeza Gibbon's national radio show and I had my own radio show "How Mama Got Her Groove Back." I loved being a Sexy Mom Expert so much that I even got up at 4 a.m. to get in line to audition for the "Hottest Mom in America" reality show. The title and identity truly served its purpose to help ignite my passion, seeing my body as art, expand my capacity for pleasure, and see it as a way to fuel my patience and playfulness as a mother.

The bottom line was that by taking the time to listen to my truth, taking good care of myself, and taking the perspective that at my core who I truly am is a sensual woman and nobody and nothing can take this God-given birthright away from me. I began to relax because I saw that it's impossible to make a mistake. We learn so much from each experience... so why NOT ooze into my succulent, juicy, radiant self... and since then I've tasted a peace that I knew was there intellectually, but had never felt in my body... and now I wish for you to know this peace and this is why I'm writing this book, you glorious mom!

Here is how my understanding of femininity began... Pink tights, black leotards, hair in an immaculate bun.

In hindsight, ballet class was an extremely confining way to move my body. Oh, how I wanted to be the Sugar Plum Fairy! I remember getting her autograph behind stage one Christmas and noticing her bleeding toes, her caked makeup, so thin and angular, void of warmth, and she wouldn't look me in the eyes. This was why I was so confused.

I remember once when I wanted to quit the Royal Conservatory of Music piano lessons, mom took me to a jazz band pianist. He asked me to play something... I went into a memorized Fugue, and he stopped me.

"NO! Make something up right now." I couldn't. I could only think in the confines of the past memorized classics. There was a void. I had no idea how the notes worked together organically. I couldn't play a thing. I ran out of there crying. I felt busted. I was so ashamed. There was nothing at my core. I had no idea who I was.

Not until my late twenties did I step foot in a free movement dance class. I hid in the corner and closed my eyes, terrified to be seen, terrified to witness others free, to witness others struggling like me. Only recently have I had the courage to face the narcissistic arrogance that I project when all I'm concerned with is how I stack up to others, how I'm looking.

Am I safe? Will I survive? Observing the truth of the craziness inside my head took a lot of courage, for it brought up waves of shame, guilt, and fear. Once through that, it brought forth forgiveness, tenderness, and compassion towards myself as I felt the degree of self-loathing that was going on. Only past the shame and past the forgiveness came the peace... the witnessing of the depth and radiance within me. It's within all of us.

This taught me that stuck feelings and stuck energy need to get moving so I've learned that dance is essential to keep my life working. I dance frequently, even swaying when I meditate, rocking my hips as I set the table for dinner. I've learned to open my chest and breathe through my heart when I connect with those I love. I've finally let go of the permanent kegel in my vagina. I allow my body to respond with stirs and warmth, or shrinking and a stomach ache. It's all guidance to direct my truth. It's been in my body all along. The answers, the joy, the peace, it's all there. I had no idea.

I had to acknowledge that I was absolutely terrified of connecting with others purely. I remember as a five-year-old girl, I would put on "Jesus Christ Superstar" and dance all around the house with my sister. I guess I hadn't heard my dad say "quiet down" for I gleefully turned the corner to go down the hall when BANG! He had punched a hole through the wall and he looked at me like I was next. I was frightened and decided in that moment that I was scared.

Scared of men, scared of life.

As an adult looking back I know he was drunk and stoned. As a little girl, all I knew was that I felt bad and unsafe, and I decided I should always be on alert. I learned to disconnect, protect, not let my guard down. I learned to become a people pleaser, to stay three steps ahead of him and everyone, to be on high alert to avoid being blindsided, and to always seek approval. I thought this approach would keep me safe. I was so in my head, spinning so quickly that it became a way of life through elementary school and high school. I didn't even know how inauthentic I was, that I hadn't exhaled, that I had this perma-smile on my face, a perma-kegel in may vagina and a perma-closure of my heart.

However, one weekend at the lake during the summer I was sixteen years old I was shown that as hard as I tried to be fast enough to outrun pain, it would eventually catch up with me.

My two friends were scheduled to arrive for a weekend visit. The first ran down the stairs, grabbed me and said, "James is dead."

I thought she was joking. Then I saw her solemn parents approach behind her. This was real. NO! As I ran up onto the highway, cars screeching as I literally ran down the yellow line looking to the tree tops of the thick pine forest begging nature to say it wasn't so, screaming,

"NO!!!!!!!"

Again, disconnect, protect, don't let your guard down.

Don't ever set yourself up to hurt like this again.

I've heard it said that, "Belief produces the acceptance of existence." I believed the world could hurt me and that it wasn't safe to relax. And lo and behold, I proved myself right, again. I was all snuggled up on the couch with my then live-in boyfriend and he told me he was moving out. Stunned, he continued, "And I've made my mind up." I said, "Stop, NO..." and proceeded to run upstairs, slamming doors, screaming "NO," jumping in the shower, bawling, hysterical, pounding the walls, screaming "NO"... until I became like an observer and saw myself reacting very similarly to the way I reacted twenty years prior when James died... knowing that what we resist persists, I gave myself permission to fully feel these feelings that I had never fully felt. I let go of concern of what my boyfriend thought, what the neighbors must be thinking, and most of all, I let go of the shame of being a hysterical wreck. I faced my demons. I faced the underlying terror that I went through life with every day. I didn't intellectually theorize about it. I felt it and WAS it. I faced it, I didn't judge it, and it dissolved.

I felt the relief of being busted. Busted that I had wanted him to save me and used him as an excuse to not move forward in my life while waiting for his to get going. I felt a rush of energy for my own career to ignite and a mature woman to step forth who knows she can more than take care of herself. That next night we made love and I think it was the first time I'd ever made LOVE. I was vulnerable, busted, real, not hiding, not pretending, not trying to get him to want me, approve of me, save me... I was simply me. It was divine.

The beauty of this challenging process of facing my fears I'd stuffed away, is that it showed me that holding onto feelings creates behaviors that push away the very thing I wanted to manifest. Feeling my feelings allowed them to dissolve and created the space for energy and life and success to flow through me again. I am beginning to master the process of alchemizing wounds into magic over and over, never getting anywhere, simply experiencing the rhythmic cycles of sorrow and bliss for their own sake. I choose life as a journey, ritually celebrating triumphs and tragedies.

It showed me that looking on the outside for approval or to be saved, also kept me away from the very love that lives inside of me. It showed me that there's nothing to do and nowhere to go and nothing to get, to feel better, happy, safe.

Love, joy, and peace live inside of me.

Believe that, be that, and only then can they be mirrored outside of me.

My experience of "how" to move my energy and my body, "how" to connect with my truth, with other women and men, is through asking.

> Asking for help with the kids.
> Asking for monthly gatherings with my mom friends.
> Asking for the perfect book to drop in my lap.
> Asking for a sacred home and community.
> Asking for the key to fitting exercise into my schedule.
> Asking for guidance from wise aunties and mentors.
> Asking for like-minded souls to grace my path.
> Asking for a deep, impeccably present life partner
> who's committed to my radiance and full expression of love.
> Asking for the courage to be grateful and open and deserving of my dream before it's manifested.

I had to be willing to ask and risk being disappointed. And I had to learn patience and trust that it might look different than what I wanted. I learned to ask and be open to something beyond my dreams. I learned to ask when I was afraid to hear the truth. I learned to ask when I was so despondent that I didn't know how to go on. I learned to ask my mom in heaven and not worry about bothering her. I learned to ask God, my

Lady, the Universe, all that is. I learned to feel connected, guided, full of faith, grateful, and in awe of this miraculous experience of life.

And in this I learned to be a better mom. Move.

Connect.

Ask.

Trust that you'll know when to reach out your hand, hold someone's hand, let go, and be still.

This undulating rhythm is inside us all.

Women, we are masters at it. Mothers truly master it. Embrace your beauty, radiate love, bestow your grace, experience the universe within you.

It follows that to be a sensual woman, a sexy mama, a radiant mother, there is nothing to do, nothing to perform, nothing to get right, or be in competition about. It's about unveiling your core nature, who you truly are naturally and organically, and stopping all the behaviors that take you out of this knowing, out of your body.

Somebody or something along the way convinced me that just being me was not enough.

That's BS.

Being produces the acceptance of existence.

Believe you are sensual. Be sensual. Move from there. Act from there. Choose from there and watch motherhood become easier, more elegant, more humbling.

We GET to be moms.

Choose to ask for help with the kids.

Choose to gather monthly with your positive, optimistic friends.

Choose for the perfect dance workshop to fit into your schedule.

Choose like-minded souls to grace your path.

Choose a deep, impeccably present partner who's committed to your radiance and full expression of love.
Choose the courage to be grateful, open, and deserving of your dream even before it's manifested.
Choose knowing you may be disappointed.
Choose knowing it may hurt to know the truth.
Choose knowing it will always be the unknown.
Choose and let go.

When I did, I found that beneath all the survival strategies, our natural state of being is connection, peace, faith, love, and sensuality. And I've become an amazing mother—human and imperfect—but amazing mother, as a result.

Embrace your beauty, radiate love, bestow your grace, take the time to experience the universe within you.

You are more than sensual, you ARE sensuality itself. You are more than a mother, you are motherhood itself. Wisdom itself. Power itself. Peace itself.

WHAT THIS MEANS FOR YOU...

What are three areas in your life in which you are going to ask for support or help?

1.

2.

3.

What are three areas of your life where you're going to stop a draining behavior?

1.

2.

3.

What nourishing behaviors will you adopt instead to replace them?

1.

2.

3.

WHY are you going to ask for help and nourish yourself? Why is it worth it even if it's challenging? Physically, mentally, emotionally, spiritually, vocationally, financially, socially, family wise, romantically, and sexually?

When you tell a NEW story and feel a NEW vibration, watch how a NEW life begins to unfold. I believe in you.

Little White Mints

I remember we thought it was hepatitis.

In line with her upbeat outlook on life, Mom wore yellow outfits to complement her jaundice. We celebrated her sixtieth birthday, all washing our hands after hugging her... insane now. It was cancer.

I remember not so much being freaked out that she would die, but rather becoming Healer with a capital H, and learning all the alternative treatments while my doctor sister handled getting Mom a slot on the operating table in Alberta because the medical system in British Columbia was too backed up to save our mom's life. Mom had a grueling fourteen-hour operation where they rewired her entire digestive system and the stitches went clear cross her body. They 'said' they got it all.

I spent the first part of mom's recovery with her in Alberta at my sister's house. I felt quite unwilling to deal with her dying at all. As far as I was concerned, she was going to be fine and stop whatever behavior or thought patterns had gotten her in this mess. I wasn't that tender, nor was I the best listener. She was going to heal God dammit and that was the end of it. Mom was remembering how her father died of cancer by the time he was fifty-four. She spoke of the anger she still held about my alcoholic father whom she'd divorced, about her mother who had disowned her. Bottled up feelings were surfacing and I began to soften up as we took slow walks in between bandage changes and sipping tea.

After a month, we headed back to Mom's home in British Columbia, and set up a "room of her own." We bought a new couch and strung Christmas lights, and she nestled into listen to healing meditation CDs. Mom dealt with her current, well-intentioned, but alcoholic boyfriend. We created a bright poster for the fridge titled "Priorities: music, travel, adventure, and laughter." She dealt with her fears of the cancer coming back. She accepted an invitation to Spain with a male friend and even took a bus tour of Amsterdam on her layover. She really started glowing. She was alive and living and the most stunning I had ever known her to be. We talked a lot. I would read her the guided meditations over the phone from LA and she'd softly repeat the affirmations.

She was on an Alaskan cruise for the May long weekend when the pain started. Afraid this was it, she cashed in her bonds and asked me to book the alternative clinic in Mexico. My sister was dead against us going. I booked the flights and rooms but got a call from Mom. She was trying to tell me she was tired. Her sister was there but she wanted me and my sister to come. She said she didn't want to fight anymore. I reamed her out, told her to keep fighting, that I would be there tomorrow morning, to hang on, that I needed her, that she wasn't allowed to die. I arrived the next morning to find her body limp. She was strung out on liquid morphine she'd been taking every two to three hours, and she couldn't lift herself out of bed, or sip water. She was burning up. My aunt was on Lord knows what number bottle of wine in the living room. I lay at the foot of my mother's bed all that night attending to her and changing cool cloths. By dawn I called the ambulance.

In the ambulance, I was asked all these specific questions. Somehow in her fog, Mom piped in with all the answers. Her blood pressure was so low that they had to administer a drug that would stabilize her at the price of taking away the pain-killing morphine. In the ER and she was moaning, screaming, and shaking with pain. I held her close and gently whispered to her to breathe with the ocean, see the calming waves, know that with every breath the pain subsides, be one with the waves, Mom, just lose yourself in the waves... I held her tight for close to thirty minutes until her body stabilized.

My sister flew in from Calgary that evening and we shared day and night shifts. Sometimes mom was sleepy and we talked with friends and family who came to visit. Sometimes mom was hysterically funny, out of nowhere yelling across the ER ward if "those damn Americans" won the hockey game. Sometimes she would get energy from God knows where and sit up in bed and ask how WE were! On the night we finally finagled her a private room, we had a lovely view of the Vancouver mountains and we three girls—me, my sister, and my mother—reminisced about our life together. As my mother tired we told her that we loved her, that we'd miss her but not to worry. We'd be just fine.

I don't know how close you've been to someone dying. They stop eating obviously, don't pee, don't talk, the nurses wash them, they have bed sores, and dry skin. I brought aromatherapy oils to rub her with and make the room smell nice. I remember once I was massaging her beautiful hands with the oil and out of nowhere she said, "No more herbs." By the end she didn't even have an IV. No more ice cubes, just a sponge to wet her lips, and bags upon bags of morphine alongside morphine boosters for nightmarish pain attacks.

I seemed to win the prize of always being there alone when crisis struck. The first painful episode upon admittance, another one when I ran up and down the halls screaming for morphine NOW as my mom was writhing in pain, but they had to order it because they can only keep so much f*&%ing morphine in the ward for security purposes. So again, I breathed every single painful breath with her until the damn stuff came.

Once when we were alone talking, she said very matter of factly, "How do I die?" I said I thought the angels came when you're ready and you go with them. She said, "Well, how do I get there? Let's make a plan. We have to figure it out. Where do we go?"

Then all of a sudden she was up, out of bed and off—morphine IV, catheter, willowy body—to go die. Trying to hold her back, she screamed at me with this high-pitched possessed voice and then bit my hand, through the skin immediately—messing with bones, veins, arteries—deep and she wasn't letting go. I was screaming, she was screaming, nurses came running and calmed her down, and now I was evil. She didn't want to ever see me again. Didn't know who I was. I was a spy sent to take her money and keep her from dying.

Holy crap! And NO ONE was sympathetic. All they could say was, "Don't be upset, she didn't mean it." *No shit, Sherlock, but it was so terrifying that I could use a little empathy here.* One aunt took me to the ER for a tetanus shot because with Mom's liver cancer, she was loaded with bacteria. To the admitting nurse, "Yes, my dying mother bit me." How humiliating, how hysterically funny in hindsight, how dearly I coveted my wound, how sad I was when the scabs fell away.

I was alone with Mom when she died. I was reading the last chapter in Joan Borysenko's *A Woman's Book of Life*. It had broken up a woman's life into seven year increments and although mom was only sixty, I was reading the last chapter when Borysenko was talking about watching her own mom die, that she saw the light in her lift and leave toward the heavens. There was a prayer at the end that I read to Mom, saying that I no longer resisted her leaving. That I was sorry it took me a little longer to accept it, but I knew she would be with me forever and that I loved her with all my heart. I put in ear plugs because she breathed like this—uuuhuuhuuhhuuh—and would stop for up to a minute at a time and then start again. Then at 5 a.m. on a beautiful, clear blue Sunday morning, the male nurse, with the same name as her father who'd died—Dave, gently woke me to say she was gone. Irritated and deaf I barked, "WHAT?" taking out my earplugs. Shit! She was gone. I missed it. The BIG moment.

Did she reach out, say something, smile, did the light float up? I'd missed it! On autopilot I called my sister and aunt at home. "She's gone." The nurse covered her head and I asked them to take the bloody sheet off, afraid to touch her at first. Then I breathed, smoothed her hair, touched her, she was already cool. I looked at her beautiful hands, her soft skin. My Mom. Laying there. Dead. Clearly she wasn't there really, just her body, but it was the body that gave birth to me, that held me, that bit me.

Family arrived and the nurse reappeared. Check out is at 9 a.m. Will she be donating her organs? Yes, yes. She wanted to do that. Whispering, we gathered all the cards. Why are we whispering? Yes, give the flowers to other people on the ward. We collected toiletries, food, and music. We were by her, leaning over her, cleaning up, and she was dead. DEAD. Then we were done. Everyone was fidgeting. I boldly gathered everyone at the end of her bed for a prayer. Then we left. We left my mother's body there. We just left. We took the same elevator down for the last time, and drove out the parking lot for the last time.

Relieved, grief-stricken, and numb we walked into the 70s décor mortuary. Is it okay to cremate her in a plywood box? Do we want something more snazzy? What style urn would we like? Would you like that shipped to LA or will my sister pick it up? Anesthetized but functioning, we found the will, planned the funeral, called everyone, changed the answering machine message, and oh, yes, drove back to Alberta in two days for my sister's wedding.

My sister and I drove alone in silence, then laughter, then streaming tears. The wedding was bittersweet. We decided to pretend mom was on vacation. My sister was courageous, bold, and vulnerable. Then we drove back to British Columbia and pulled up to our dead mother's condo. We hosted over 100 people to a beautiful afternoon tea in our mother's honor at the Botanical Gardens. Over the next few weeks we drank a lot, ate up all the food in her fridge as we packed up her life and put her condo on the market.

Packing up was wild. She had little white mints in nearly all her pockets. She kept EVERY letter and card I ever sent her in a Rice Krispies box. And she had more sex toys than I'm comfortable mentioning. Oh, and they took her eyes. Funny thing though because mom had laser surgery and they corrected one eye for bifocals and one eye for long distance.

Oh, and I was pregnant. It happened at my sister's wedding before the funeral.

WHAT THIS MEANS FOR YOU...

How are you with death?

Have you lost a parent? Both? Neither? How are you with feeling your feelings?

Embracing your fears?

Being tender with yourself when you're afraid? Asking for support when you need it?

Take this time to journal the truth about losing your parents. If one or both are gone, journal a letter to them as if you're really talking to them, for I believe they can hear. See if by the end you can taste the truth of what I believe, which is we never die, just change forms. And that we chose our parents for the very best environment from which we could lose ourselves, and then find ourselves and soar into our most authentic selves.

Next, after you've journaled to your parents... I want to share with you the first short story I ever published in an anthology called *Thank God I*.

"Thank God I'm a Single, Motherless Mom"

A decrepit, rotting witch, crazy gray hair astray, pointed her bony finger at me. "You weak waste of life!" Desperate, I pleaded my case. "But I have an infant. I can't sleep. My mom just died. I'm not working. I'm supporting my unemployed husband on her inheritance... and you want me to leave?" Hunched over, she turned away, chuckling, "Your son knows you're a wimp. A loser."

Infuriated, I felt a dormant power deep within me rise up, and I screamed, "Fine! I'll jump off the cliff! Not another day will pass letting my son see his mother void of power and grace!" The witch turned, cunningly smiled, and transformed before my eyes into Xena, Warrior Princess. "I was worried you'd never come around, sister. We've got work to do. Know I am a part of you. Kick him out. Now."

Talk about a powerful meditation! I barely slept that night, rigid and boiling, beside the man to whom I'd given away all my power. The next morning I fed my son, stormed downstairs, blared Gypsy Kings, and screamed at the top of my lungs, "You're going down. Get out now!"

No more believing his accusations that I was crazy. No more paying his way. No more putting up with his manipulations, threats, pushing me, then calling the cops to say I attacked him. No more insanity. No more hiding my power. No more buying into this victim story that drained my energy, withholding joy, grace, and radiance from my son.

Why had I stayed so long? Why did I feel so powerless? My inner warrior had only just begun to awaken when my mom had died.

Now not only was she my angel, so was Xena the Warrior Princess! It was time for healing and action. I forgave myself (multiple times daily, at first). I put affirmation sticky notes around the house, asked for help with financial issues, told the truth of how scared I was, got coaching on my career, dressed confidently, and exercised. I danced a few nights a week by candlelight, once my son was asleep for the night. I faced the truth of how needy I still felt, how I wanted a man to save me, an investment to sustain me, something on the outside to make the pain on the inside go away.

I started dating and vowed to tell the truth, be myself, explore my true sensual expression, and never settle again. Slowly, I began to live sensually, in the moment, savoring life more deeply and cherishing motherhood. I felt this unexplainable, unconditional love for my son that healed the loss of my mom, for I knew the depth to which she had really loved me.

WHAT THIS MEANS FOR YOU...
I invite you to write your own "Thank God I..." story. What lead are you ready to alchemize into gold?
What challenge are you ready to say "THANK YOU" for?
Bonus: read your story to a trusted friend, post it on your blog, read it to your beloved. SHARE your inner most truth. Be bold and vulnerable and LET GO.

My Portal to Freedom

We swirl our fingers through luscious shaving cream on the bright red picnic table. This lasts barely a minute before my soapy toddler and I are in a full-fledged foam fight. We artfully compare our sudsy mohawks, rinse off, and retire for a restorative nap. His trumpeting voice alerts me that he's ready to race into the afternoon, so crouching down on all fours, I enter the room clucking like a chicken. He laughs hysterically as I beam.

Maybe it was giving birth and spreading my legs for all to see that dismantled my preoccupation with what people thought of me. Until the birth of my son, I was wired to seek approval for my every decision. Disapproval felt like fingernails down a chalkboard. I remember the shame of being turned away by my former husband, too preoccupied with work to enjoy my surprise lunchtime strip tease. I remember women's glances of pity as I, the poor girl who hadn't the pedigree to know any better, chatted and tore open my power bar for a homeless, fingerless man.

I valued other's approval more than my own eroticism or generosity. The insecure lens through which I saw the world opened, literally, during birth. My thoughts and behaviors were molding an innocent human being. I had been waiting for permission to stop flat-lining through life. Motherhood became my portal to freedom.

My own mother once told me, "You wouldn't care so much about what people think of you if you knew how little they did." At the local diner her wisdom comforted me as my son smashed eggs and hash browns into his hair then plopped into the public fountain. I was reminded that he was washable. Dryable. I encouraged myself to savor these tender moments.

From my new vantage point, it turns out dirt is decadent, mess is marvelous, and hugging trees is grand. My creativity abounded as we picnicked in the backyard tree house, read under forts of blankets, napped in tents in his room. My brain said, *I don't have the time or energy for this silliness!* But my heart whispered, "nourish and liberate your soul to the brim with sticky hands and make-believe."

This latitude spilled over into juicy girlfriend time. Instead of victim sessions over the phone, we had fun painting each other's toes in the driveway at sunset and dining by candlelight on the shag rug around the coffee table. Conversations were magical, laughter was intoxicating, and insights were divinely inspired. I was still pissy on my period, beside myself when my kid clobbered another kid, and angry when drivers cut me off, yet these moods passed quickly because I could now see joy was my choice, my responsibility, my gift to myself.

Being able to lovingly laugh at myself through the process sustained that joy. Bless motherhood for pouring forth my wellspring of happiness.

Let's just hope my son forgets that I clucked like a chicken.

Actually, let's hope not!

WHAT THIS MEANS FOR YOU...

How silly are you? Goofy are you?

Free are you? Expressed are you?

I invite you to do one silly thing a day. Downright dorky, Divine Dorkiness.

See where your comfort zone is and go beyond. Ask your kids for ideas and the VERY thing you least want to do, do that one!

Stretch your edges, laugh until your sides hurt, let go of what people think.

Know I adore you, and so do your kids for unleashing this energy.

Part 2: The Babe You Are...

Addiction to Frustration

You mean I can't blame my ex-husband for everything?

What's absolutely imperative that I share with you as a mother is my take on anger. And self-pity. And my absolute certainty that everything was my ex-husband's fault.

I believe unexpressed anger and unclaimed self-pity could be the biggest single most destructive, draining force that thwarts you having the most enjoyable successful and meaningful motherhood ever. I had a part-time job blaming my ex for all my struggles.

When as moms we live in emptiness, not taking care of ourselves physically and emotionally, we can easily slip into entitlement, expectations, poor me, and self-pity.

When as moms we live in fullness, filling up our tanks physically, tending to our emotions, and following their guidance, we are able to receive support from the universe, we are able to celebrate the journey... this is really important, sisters!

Thus, take a breath. This is intense.

It's quite vulnerable for me to share, and a bitter pill to swallow if it resonates with you. So hang in there...

Do you know what NO MOM, (in my opinion), is allowed to feel and express... at least openly, or she'll be shamed? ANGER.

Anger at no longer having freedom, no longer having eight hours to sleep, no longer having two hours to primp, or a body that's her own anymore.

Anger that she's got a body whose organs are rearranged so she looks and feels bloated all the time.

Anger, or feeling completely at a loss, of what to do to make them stop crying,

or hitting kids at school or hanging out with the wrong crowd,

or extra weight that's a pisser to release even after they're ten-years-old which makes you feel less than sexy,

or all the demands put on you to be super woman, and do it with a smile... because YOU are lucky enough to have kids!

Sure we complain about it.

Sure we might leak out a little victim banter about it. Sure we might cry about it.

But heaven forbid we actually get angry! We should be grateful we even have kids!

We should remember that women don't get angry, especially about innocent little kids!

Instead of expressing it, anger lays dormant, then grows, doubles in size, and then takes the form of exhaustion, depression, lack of libido, competition with other moms, insecurity about our sexual attractiveness, indecisiveness about our dreams and visions, insane doubting if our partner desires us, and instantly losing our patience at the smallest infraction from the kids.

It's simply bad manners to ever really release your anger in a healthy way, and let 'er rip!

And over time, that anger grows so huge that it's downright terrifying to consider letting 'er rip because it feels like you would eat Jupiter for breakfast in your rage.

So you stuff it. Stuff it.

And it extinguishes your radiance, lusciousness, capacity to be sensual, creative, and magnetic.

A shield of protection builds around your power center, covering your heart, locking off your pelvis, giving you that "edge" of curtness, do do do, ready to blow any second, pushing to get it all done, unwilling to feel a damn thing.

You've seen these moms. You may be her right now.

Your solution is to give yourself permission to value and express your anger, in a healthy manner, just as you would have a good laugh or a good cry. Time for a good rant.

If you don't, it quickly mutates into self-pity.

(poor me) that I don't sleep all night and haven't for years.
(poor me) that I don't feel sensual, sexy, and satisfied with my femininity and marriage.
(poor me) that she has a nanny, and her husband takes the kids so she can go to yoga.
(poor me) that I'm too exhausted to go to yoga even if I could.
(poor me) I think I'll just medicate myself with drugs, alcohol, and exercise non-stop, shopping 'til I drop, volunteering 'til no one notices, especially me, that I'm dying inside.

This is not a pretty picture, I know.

And this was ME, ME, ME until I was willing to tell the

truth and take responsibility for expressing and releasing my anger at my Dad, Mom, ex-husband, life, God, and the Goddess even.

I had so many layers of victim, poor me tears and terrifying rage and anger stuck inside me.

I was the martyr big time, struggling with my happy face— a single, motherless mom, grateful for all the lessons, focusing on the good, exhausted and angry at the world that it was so hard for me... denying the full expression of that anger with my Pollyanna Kumbaya happy time talk about how grateful I am.

YES, I AM GRATEFUL.

AND I WAS F'ING ANGRY!

AND I WAS HAVING A SILENT PITY PARTY ABOUT IT EACH TIME ANOTHER SHOE DROPPED!

Don't worry, the whole book isn't about this. You'll be having more fun in a minute. I just need you to really take this to heart. Your family, marriage, sensuality, sex life, self-esteem, and sanity are at risk.

And my mom died at sixty from cancer of the liver. Anger ate her alive.

You still have a choice. And when the anger is gone, there will probably be sobs of grief, unexpressed sadness. Let it ALL out and trust that you can set it all free and be open, light, expanded, present, self-forgiving, forgiving of all, and free to enjoy motherhood and create the life of your dreams.

WHAT THIS MEANS FOR YOU...

Create time for YOU one night and take out your trusted journal.

At the top, state: I am angry about... and start writing. Pages.

Cry if you need to, scream into a pillow if you need to, just get it out.

When you're done, read it to yourself. Really let it out.

Then on day two, read it again and see if you're being a victim of your circumstances, a struggler, whiner, blamer, competitive, martyr, self-pitying, or fake happy face mom. If you find any self-pity, and chances are we ALL will find some, make the decision to change your point of view. Instead choose to respond to your circumstances as a winner would, as a victorious diva would, as a queen would, as a high priestess would. Get back in your chariot. Take back the reigns. No one has power over you. You are a conscious being of choice... and you can create your own point of view of what happened.

Call a friend who's a 'successful' mom and talk to her about it. Take my Intimacy Blindspot Assessment quiz to discover what's in the way of you letting it go quiz. Don't stuff it down, beautiful. Don't pretend you're fine when you're not. Too much is at stake. You, amazing woman, are worth it. And being free of the poison and toxic energy of anger feels sooooooooooo good when you transform it into compassion and divine action toward your dreams!

Momnesia: Who Am I Anyway?

Forgetfulness during pregnancy was cute. Yet, why hadn't my sharpness and wit and confidence returned now that I was a mother?

Why was I feeling ashamed and stumbling over my words when asked the question, "What do you do?"

I had no idea that becoming a mom—the greatest thing that's ever happened to me—would mean losing my sense of self, my identity. Am I a mom, a wife, a career woman with dreams? Or a machine that feeds the family and forgets her soul? I knew I was having a victim moment, but some days it felt like I gave so much and never fueled back up, never quite relaxed enough to exhale fully.

I don't know about you, but when I don't take care of myself I become crabby and it's everyone else's fault. My ex-husband would probably say I become a controlling bitch.

When I looked in the mirror at all that excess ME, I became insecure (which also showed up as controlling bitch). And when there was no paycheck or thank you for working my butt off changing diapers, I felt worthless (another expression of controlling bitch). I felt taken for granted, envious of others, and overlooked. When my son was six weeks old, I lost it and checked into a hotel for two nights. I never left the room, just slept, pumped, and cried.

I had watched my mom sacrifice her life to be the codependent caretaker for my drug-abusing, alcoholic father. So I had no clue I was even allowed to take time for myself, let alone know how to nourish my soul. I didn't put it together that if I was depleted that I couldn't be the mother and wife I wanted to be. All I thought about was that I would be selfishly neglecting my family and people would think I was a shallow, incapable mother.

I found out the hard way that not taking care of myself, being a victim to my situation, and being crabby all the time, did not a marriage make. Nor did it make me very happy. I was a divorced, single mom by the time my son was one. I would enviously see women in the super market, patient with their kids, in shape, dressed in the latest fashions, talking to their sweeties on the cell. How did they do it? I knew that being a victim about my situation was not the route to finding the answer. So instead of hating these women, I breathed and chose to see these women as my teachers, directing me toward another way of life.

Funny how forgiveness can shift perspectives and change everything. Some deep feelings inside me woke up, reminding me that I too deserved to feel radiant, sensual, and alive. Reminding me that I could stop a generational pattern of women who gave everything and received nothing, only to die unhappy, early, and with potential still intact, never knowing what living a thriving, flourishing life was like.

Thank you, hot mamas in the grocery store for waking me up, because after my mom's death, the new baby, and then the divorce, I was listening.

I wanted nothing more than to be at peace and free to be me so that I could BE a great mom: one who was a powerful, graceful, and inspiring woman.

I'm still a work in progress.

I've had many a challenge. I still get zits during my period even though I'm friggin' fifty, yet I courageously took an erotic dance class so I can be in love with every inch of my body. As for the ex, truth is, in the beginning I prayed for some mafioso to somehow remove him from this plane of existence. But after a while that prayer didn't feel very good so I prayed for him to have a great job and a great woman so he'd be happy, to be a great dad, and to be easy to get along with. I wish him well.

Bottom line is that it's my honor and joy to teach moms how to have the energy, the mindset, and the heart space to be more playful with their kids, more ravishing with their men, more nurtured by their friends, and more shining in their careers.

I know the study of being a sexy mom may seem fanciful or irrelevant, but nourishing myself with a forty-eight minute coffee with my best friend, a thirty-six minute pedicure, or even a seven minute quickie with myself translates into me being a happy mom. Happy moms have thriving relationships and flourishing families. Even in the midst of carpooling, diapers, or homework, I believe the universe will support us to be sensual goddesses, radiant lights, luminous healers. We simply have to ask. And we also need to know we deserve it.

Sure I lose it on occasion, but I also make a point of dancing on the coffee table with my son, having nights at a hotel so I can moan in ecstasy at any volume, and I'm not stopped by my fear of disappointing others when I say "No" to an event, and "Yes" to a bubble bath.

I can honestly say my life works now. I'm living proof that **When Mama's Happy, Everybody's Happy.** And it came from valuing myself exactly as I am.

WHAT THIS MEANS FOR YOU...

Do one thing differently today, Mama.

Take five extra minutes to do what makes you feel pretty. Move your body even as you set the table.

Ask for help instead of heavy sighing and doing it all yourself.

Be silly with the kids and have a water fight.

Pull out that sexy lingerie tonight and choose to be more open than you ever have to experiencing deep pleasure for exactly who you are.

Most importantly, breathe. Life is good, Friends.

And YOU are so appreciated on this planet for being exactly who you are.

Challenges That, Well, Challenge Me About Motherhood

OVERREACTING

As moms we really are sooooooo busy! We are fitting not double, but triple the responsibilities in our time (hubby plus child plus us equals three!) Compound that with some guilt and it results in rarely taking time to listen deeply to how we are truly feeling. Instead we use unrelated disappointments here and there to really unload our grievances. My sister calls it "zero to sixty" where she's fine, fine, fine, fine, then BLOWS. My advice would be to do whatever it takes (like ask for help) and create a standing non-negotiable appointment with yourself—let's say a bubble bath once a week—and check in. Do you need to really cry? Do you want to journal if you're confused? Do you want to write some creative thoughts down? Do you want to stop thinking and simply BE? We all have the same twenty-four hours a day. If you don't schedule YOU time, it doesn't happen and that inner voice can't guide and encourage you. NO more excuses. You're worth it!

When I coached Leeza Gibbons, this was the practice she had already figured out brilliantly. She's a bath queen and it's her time to go within. She's also an avid hiker. Up the mountain, ask her questions. Down the mountain, let it all go and listen for guidance. She walks her talk.

TANTRUMS

To be a sensual woman in the face of chaos—it takes a lot. Especially in the grocery store as your child flails himself like a whirling Tasmanian devil, crashing down several brands of cereal boxes all over the aisle... and yet see if you can breathe, see if you cannot glare. See if you cannot grab your child and threaten them (believe me I've done all this). Instead, and this takes practice—breathe and open your heart no matter what's happening. I know we've been raised to care about what people think of us, but for the moment, suspend time and stay present with your child. In that moment, instead of judging, resisting, and reacting to outside judgments, open, breathe, and affirm that YOU CAN HANDLE IT. I find that validating them and expressing understanding really works. "Wow, you seem really upset. Hmmm, you seem frustrated." Breathe and know that inside is your intuition, and you can't go wrong from a place of love. You'll be amazed at the creative solutions you find once they realize that melting down doesn't faze you.

WANDERING EYES

Let's say you are a new mom, perhaps your breasts are still leaking when you hear any child in the vicinity cry, perhaps you're still carrying some baby weight, grateful to be out with your man for a date, even have some makeup on, even had a shower! Yet you're still not feeling HOT. Then a beautiful woman walks by and you watch his eyes stray. You haven't slept well in months, you haven't had time for you in forever, and inside you are either boiling or destroyed.

I get it. Ouch. You KNOW what will happen if you glare, if you whine, or if you stuff it inside. Been there, done that. What if in that moment, you opened? What if you actually took the dagger out of her back or his back and said, "Thank you." Crazy, I know but stay with me.

Let's consider that she is your mirror. You are a radiant woman, too. Let her remind you that you are a piece of ART as well and she's a powerful reminder to take even BETTER care of yourself. Perhaps it's time to ask for help, get back to the gym, make your mom time a priority. See if instead of stuffing the anger which will poison you, if you can forgive him, forgive her, and simply love yourself exactly where you are and breathe. If we shut down and get snippy, we know how the evening will go.

Instead, open, shine, and watch how your husband responds to you the rest of the evening. I invite you instead to simply share your honest vulnerable truth. I bet the two of you will get closer and I bet he'll be mesmerized by your courage, strength, and radiance.

STUFFINESS

I used to think silly was, well, silly. I was so conditioned to look outside of myself for validation and acceptance that I never relaxed and let it all hang out. Now I think silly is sexy. I think dorky is delicious. Now, I did want to raise a well-mannered boy and yet in the midst of all my rules, there needed to be some silliness for my son to go wild and for me to let go! We liked to dance on our coffee table to reggae. We'd go to the grocery store in our pajamas or to the Santa Monica Pier in costumes when it wasn't Halloween! (You may have seen the video of me as Swamp Queen with a green wig?) We'd have dinner in the playhouse or under the table in a fort and eat mac and cheese with our fingers. One time we had a shaving cream fight in the back yard and washed off in the kiddy pool. Sometimes I'd make two sippy cups, one with juice for him and one adult-style for me! Apparently, men find me sexy when I'm free with my son. You see, sexy is being free and at peace in your body. Loving your self and the moment exactly as it is. They translate it into us being free in bed, open to the unknown, a YES to life. All of those things make men admire and be inspired and turned on by us. So loosen up and have some fun! Let your kids bring out YOUR inner child who needs to play too!

WHAT THIS MEANS FOR YOU...

What irks you about motherhood?
I know we're supposed to be all positive, the law of attrac-

tion and all that, and I believe that what you focus on expands, and yet what you resist persists, too! I've coached so many moms who say, "I'm fine," then within two minutes they're in tears.

What are you covering up, love? Stuffing down? Denying? When you shine light on it, only THEN can you change it!

When you look at it with compassion, you will see it for what I really is and be able to make a shift.

Too scary? For goodness sake, join our group coaching series. It honestly feels amazing to know you're not alone, you're not weird, and things won't be this way forever. XOXOXO.

Relax and Enjoy the Crisis

When our kids were young, my amazing sister and family were in town for four days on their way from Canada to Mexico. We used to see each other about twice a year. We're both moms. Hers were eight months, two and three. Mine was five. The first night the three older kids, her husband, my boyfriend at the time, and my ex-husband all went out to a hockey game while I had a girl's night with my sis and the baby. Pretty cool.

The second night of their stay at 11:30 p.m., I heard a panicked, "MOMMM!!" My son had projectile vomited all over himself and the bed. Poor muffin. By 5:30 a.m. I had been up, tended to him, changed his clothes and sheets SEVEN times. I was using table cloths for sheets. By 9 a.m., the eight-month-old began to throw up, and I was devastated. I felt like crap, I was cranky, impatient, and pissed off that my short time to see my sister was ruined.

Or was it?

Could I relax and enjoy the crisis?

We've all been there in some fashion when we're at our wits

end AND it's the holidays and we want everything to be perfect while all the family dynamics are pushing our buttons! After feeling really sorry for myself, I remembered I always have a choice.

Allana, embrace the moment. Breathe into the moment.

Breathe into the area in my body that I'm holding my tension. Stop resisting exactly what's happening.

It is what it is. Plans have changed.

Forgive myself, others, the moment, and breathe. Let the humor of it all bubble up.

By simply allowing myself to stop resisting, my disappointment and frustration could dissolve and I had half a chance at being sane. As soon as I accepted what was, I received a huge boost of energy that I must have been draining from being pissed off. This boost of energy lifted me to a new vantage point from which I saw my situation through new eyes.

I could actually LAUGH.

My sister and I began to find humor in it and said it was that instead of adventures through the city, we were having adventures in laundry. Night three as we put our fourth load of laundry into the washer, we broke out some wine, a deck of cards, lit candles, and began to play Crazy 8's and Rummy as we did when we were kids at the lake in the cabin on a rainy summer's night. We might never have reminisced, connected deeply, or remembered the simple pleasures in life had our kids not gotten sick. We didn't strive to do enough or be enough or do it right. We simply relaxed and breathed into our situation.

No matter what crazy or annoying dynamics unfold for you, honor yourself by feeling your feelings and then embrace exactly where you are. Breathe, forgive, and be open to creativity and humor as you allow a fresh perspective to unfold. Like me, you may fall more in love with your sister while folding record loads of laundry.

WHAT THIS MEANS FOR YOU...

Remember a time when life gave you a major challenge and you lost it. You reacted and didn't respond. You lost it. Bit some heads off, punished yourself.

Now breathhhhhhhhheeeeeee. I want you to remember the lesson we just learned.

You CAN handle it.

You ARE wise, calm, safe, and good. Now rerun that scene in your mind.

Go up and whisper to your old self a new solution.

Whisper a new perspective, a new practice for dealing with challenges.

Now replay the scene with yourself choosing another response.

Watch how elegantly you handle it. Watch how you use humor.

Watch how everyone else responded differently as well. Feel the feelings of a job well done.

Feel the feelings of being proud of yourself of how far you've come.

Now make THAT your only memory of that situation. And so it is.

Struggle is Optional

When a mom lives in her head, as I exhaustingly did for so many years, she only has access to the files of the past stored in her brilliant mind... impressive, strategic initiatives that once conquered worlds. Given that they succeeded in the past, when she is presented (love that word "presented" because it drives home that the fact that the only moment we have IS the present moment) with a challenge... if she only looks in her mind to the past to solve it... she is setting herself up for struggle, panicked control, aggressive, forceful trying, even manipulation. She is certainly creating attachment to the result, fueled by sheer blind will.

In turning her attention away from NOW and looking to the past for a solution, the present moment and all limitless possibility is passing her by. She wonders why she gets so exhausted trying to make something happen as she applies yesterday's strategies to today's challenges. The frustration only makes her push harder and get more exhausted, which dissolves her faith and deepens her fear and resignation that "once again she has to do it all herself."

THIS WAS MY LIFE!!!!!!!!! Until I learned to move through times of challenge with pleasure as I sat in the fire.

This is when we get out of our head and into our hearts through courage, persistence, and fierce love of self, to stop the struggle and let go.

Letting go takes strength!

It requires us to greet the present moment like a warrior goddess, with an open heart and listening body... not a busy mind scrambling for some strategy that may have worked before.

When we sit in the fire, in that sweet spot between surrender and showing up, solutions are garnered from the great unknown, found through listening to our intuition, through accessing our feminine power, and allowing guidance to part the waters and show us the way.

Instead of spinning, you can simply choose to stop, feel, breathe, and be.

Before I began to BE in the moment and sit sizzling in the fire of the challenge, I was terrified not to addictively apply a strategy, run away, or defend myself. I didn't have the courage to sit in the unknown and listen, to trust myself, to trust God, to trust that everything was actually unfolding as it's meant to. I didn't know how to listen to my highest truth.

What if God let me down and wasn't there? I wondered.

In yoga, have you ever experienced a pose that is so painful yet you surrender and it's almost delicious because you're so stretched, so open, so willing, that magically you feel supported by a force you didn't know was there? I had no prior experience of myself as that powerful, that expansive, that vast, that free. In surrender, I could begin to touch the edges of my delicious immensity.

Now, at a time when I feel challenged, I get out of my head, breathe into the challenge, and surrender into the pleasure of the present moment. It takes courage and persistence, yet if I keep breathing and trust, I sink wide and deep and open to a place where I can't be hurt, can't be swayed, can't be manipulated. I sit like a queen on my throne, reigning over my kingdom, savoring the moment of my soul expanding, cherishing the discomfort of breathing into the void. And I find I am limitless. From this place truth is my balanced partner. I can move mountains, thrive through diversity, flow through challenge, shine with persistence, savor my power, and ultimately leave a legacy of what true feminine power is in service to this world.

Sweet mom sisters, from the most humble place where I tell you how crazy I've been, I invite you to trust me on this one as I trusted the ones who invited me.

Consciousness shifts when we surrender into our feminine power.

Feminine power helps you sit in the fire and burn away the spinning to find your truth.

Trust, breathe, open, let go, and know the truth of who you really are.

Ride the wave of pleasure through the present moment as you feel safe, held, and ONE with all.

Allow parenting to become the most challenging, delicious joy of your life.

WHAT THIS MEANS FOR YOU...

What are you resisting? Take a moment now.

Where in your body are you holding it? Nervousness, anxiety, a contraction, constriction? Not the story, just the feeling.

Breathe into it.

See if you can stay with it, with your breath, allow it.

Let thoughts go and just focus on the feeling. Give it a color, shape, size, maybe it's a little you. Let this energy or person speak.

What do they want you to know? Whatever they say, don't argue, just get it. Say "thank you, tell me more" and listen.

Stay in the feeling, not the thoughts, listen to the feeling talking.

Great wisdom will be revealed.

Give it what it needs: validation, understanding, being heard, being gotten.

Breathe. Something will have shifted.

You will have dropped deeper into your power. Soon you will touch peace beyond words.

It's in there, it's in everyone. Repeat as necessary.

I repeat daily, sometimes many times daily. This practice is your ally.

It's the most self-loving thing you can do. Love ALL of you, not just the pretty parts.

Part 3:
The Babe You Will Be...

It's Time to Teach

I want to share an experience with you, the very one that compelled me to write my first book, begin products, really step out there speaking, putting my work online, and getting out of my own way.

I was at a workshop for love, relationships and sexuality. Without giving away the practices of the workshop, suffice it to say that women, just by standing there, not saying a word, eyes closed, give men the opportunity to decide if they'd like to sleep with us or not, and if they believe we would take them to God and keep them on purpose if they were alone with us on a desert island for twenty years... or not. Some women are neither, some one or the other, and only one was both—me. Whoa. Breathe. Feeling honored, concerned the other women wouldn't like me, turned on, humbled, freaked out that this means I'm actually walking my talk and I'm being called out to step up and give to my community what I've learned.

Did this really just happen? The men chose me to want to

sleep with. I'm dressed in a loose blouse, no tits showing, long sweater, funky earrings, crazy hair, and cowboy boots beside Miss Hottie, gorgeous, twenty years younger with a body I'd love to have... wild. AND these men trusted me to hold them to their purpose and take them to God if they were alone with me on a desert island for twenty years. In fact many women chose me too!

I could feel my ego battling. Look gracious and say, "No, no, no," then, "Yes, yes, yes... you really are enough!" The mind is so amazing! It really was a brief moment where I had compassion for actors/speakers/politicians/etc. who can get lost in the illusion that they are better, misuse their power, feed off the praise. I grounded myself. What's wild is that I felt this huge buzz in my breasts and nipples to keep shining from my feminine nourishing self. Bizarre, but it helped me stay so present and I truly had the experience of being used by God for the exercise... of giving over my body, mind, and soul for the highest good of the group.

For over an hour of conversation, we dissected my beingness that attracted those votes. I even graciously added to the workshop leader's insights and interacted with the seminar attendees, especially this one women still holding onto anger. I remember it like it was yesterday. She was told to go and hit some pillows to disperse this anger. Good and yet what could we do for her in this moment? She was instructed to say, "Fuck You!" to men. She did her best yet sounded like a scared mouse. I guided her to say it from her womb, the depths of her being, her vulva lips, from the depths of the grand canyon within her. Holy shit! She transformed. Shook the room. Cried. Healed. Stunning.

I sat down, feeling almost out of my body yet tremendously grounded, and in another dimension all at the same time. And I cried. I had shown up. I had served. I was ready.

Just then a woman came to sit with me and looked deep into my heart. All she said was, "It's time to teach."

It was one of the most expansive and humbling moments of my life. That all my hard work, therapy, workshops, dancing, journaling, praying, the divorces, the deaths... it had all paid off because now I was worthy of teaching another. The responsibility was massive. The honor was humbling. And it is from this place I share what I learned.

And so moms, when we can be sexy (in its most sacred sense) and inspire a man to live his purpose, let's just say it contributes to friggin' awesome marriages and nourishes the kids big time. AND it empowers YOU to live in your sensual power, feeling confident, vibrant, peaceful, and free.

First, about having men want to sleep with you.

Of course we're really interested in YOUR man wanting to sleep with you, but a little attention here and there reminds him what a goddess he has, yes? Ha. So, I ask you, do you think I am sexy to get mens' validation or attention? No. Honestly, I used to do that in my insecure days and would attract men who only wanted my body as a piece of meat, not my heart. Second, do I show up this way for my own self-confidence to prove to myself I am enough? Nope. Interestingly enough, I used to be this way and I attracted men who wanted to pay half at dinner, who didn't make me and my son a priority, who only showed up if I showed up, tit for tat, you know. Third, did I show up this way because I'm committed to savoring life itself, moment to moment, inhaling the pleasure of being alive as a woman, and letting bliss have its way with me as a willing vessel of light for the planet? Yes. I mean, I don't consciously say it like that 24/7 but I do FEEL that whenever I am conscious of it. I used to be afraid that showing up for the sake of showing up wouldn't get me what I needed, wouldn't make me safe, wouldn't let me be in control, wouldn't allow me to rest. Now

I see it's the ONLY way to be peaceful and supported and receive more than I've ever dreamed of!!!

So to review, if you're feeling unappreciated, as we moms can easily feel when we do EVERYTHING to keep life and kids afloat... If you try to be radiant to get his attention or to feel enough, then you will look and feel like a manipulator, and potentially push away the very attention and appreciation you are seeking. If you're concerned and hide your radiance so as not to be competitive or outshine other women, or you convince yourself that being sexy doesn't matter anymore, you may actually come across as arrogant, withholding, or disgruntled, and thus a man won't trust that it's safe to touch you, praise you, or comfort you. The only way to attract a man who will ravish and honor you (and magnetize girlfriends who will celebrate the best in you) is to be radiant for the sake of experiencing radiance itself as YOU... in moment to moment divine union with spirit in your body, in the now. In this place you are so magnetic, you take his breath away, you are light itself, beauty itself, love itself. From this place it is the most effective energy to ask for what you need. From fullness, a request is a delicious invitation to serve a queen.

So now let's get deeper into the HOW.

How do I entice a man to want to sleep with me when I'm focused on delicious bodily union with the divine? I experience pleasure in my body for the sake of experiencing pleasure in my body, not for any external reason whatsoever.

I enjoy breathing fully, as if to breathe in the sun, the trees, music, smells, the moment. I enjoy being in my body and I dance regularly to release any shame stuck there, any anger, any betrayal, any insecurity. I cry almost every time I dance. Still. It's as if as I move throughout life to the grocery store or to my son's t-ball practice, I feel the air press into me and meet it like I would meet my lover. The breeze, the temperature, my clothes against my skin. I take it all in for the pleasure of sensation itself. Yes it's a little nutty in the beginning, but it's a hell of a lot better than staying up in my doubtful mind questioning my worth and dreaming up my demise!!!

I also meet emotions or circumstances this way—even uncomfortable ones—I breathe INTO conflict and experience my emotions without having to shut them down. This takes practice as sometimes I have felt like my emotions would overtake me, eat me up, make me lose consciousness, or make me insane. Thus I breathe into uncertainty and the unknown and meet it with the courage of a spiritual warrior, confident that I can handle anything because I'm not alone. I'm an open vessel for spirit to animate me, guide me, support me, love me, and shepherd me to the highest choice for all. I imagine (and look forward to the day when I can actually see) thousands of angels all around me, supporting me. And all this apparently made a then 38-year-old single mother wearing jeans, cowboy boots and a baggy Indian tunic the one they wanted to sleep with. Go figure.

Really let that sink in... because the media wants us to believe one definition of sexy. Now you know the truth.

Next, there are two factors that make a man trust you to take him to God and hold him on purpose. The first is to your open heart. My heart closed when little Jimmy didn't want to kiss me one summer when I was ten. It closed again when my first steady boyfriend in high school, the one I wanted to lose my virginity to, ended up sleeping with some other more promiscuous woman at a party after dating me for two years and I had to find out through gossip at school. My heart closed when my friend died abruptly in a car accident when I was sixteen. Certainly during both my divorces, numerous other occasions when someone betrayed me, fired me, died on me, I closed my heart.

And the same is true for you, right?

So how in the world are we supposed to open our hearts for a man? Well, in my experience, don't open it for him. He'll end up hurting you at some point even if he's wonderful because he's human, just like we are. Don't open your heart to heal or get better and be done with it all. Now, while I encourage self-forgiveness of course, the reason I say don't open your heart to simply heal, is that there's still an agenda in parenthesis. Because who you are and how you are ISN'T OKAY dammit, it's a high-level manipulation to get rid of the pain and to get the guy to love you and get the attention you seek. It's only an abbreviated cure because as soon as you get let down again, your heart will be hurt again and you'll be in constant therapy.

Thus, in my experience, the only pure lasting way to open your heart is to open it for the sake of experiencing what an open heart is like ... not to feel better. An open heart hurts sometimes—sorry to break the news—yet we both know a closed heart hurts more. Only an open heart opened for the sake of experiencing ecstasy AND pain, triumph AND tragedy, bliss AND betrayal, cannot be manipulated. Only this open heart tells the truth no matter what another has to say about you. Only this open heart welcomes in oneness with all that is, because it knows it IS all that is. As everything, limitless consciousness, and love, your open heart is simultaneously creating and living in this realm while surrendering and being guided by the inspiration of God. And an open heart allows for emotions to be welcomed as guide posts. An open heart can't be swayed by the fear of disappointing another or being disappointed. It will feel all that is.

This is HUGE as a mother! Huge! You know how wonderful it feels the first time your child says, "I love you." And you know how awful it feels the first time they say, "I hate you." You know how wonderful it feels to see your partner living their purpose, and you know how devastating and painful it is to see them floundering.

A good man is attracted to this open heart because it will not shy away if in pain, sorrow, or fear. It will stay open and express the pain, sorrow, or fear which demands of him his nobleness, his highest integrity, his truest support. What if he loses his job? The stock market crashes? The investment goes south? He makes a mistake? Gets sick? A heart that closes from pain, sorrow, or fear, will bark at him, withhold from him, blame and project onto him, emasculate him. Obviously not attractive. So open your heart, not FOR him, or even for your identity, but for experiencing all that an open heart can feel. And know that the gorgeous byproduct is that you will attract the most noble qualities in your man, a man worthy of your glorious heart.

Now, the last way to attract your man, who will trust you to take him to God and hold him on purpose, is to have your Kali alive. Kali is the destructive and devouring Hindu goddess of death and destruction, depicted as black, red-eyed, blood-stained, and wearing a necklace of skulls. Kali is commonly associated with violence, sexuality, and, paradoxically, with motherly love. In her four hands she holds, variously, a sword, a shield, the severed head of a giant, or a noose for strangling. She is often shown standing or dancing on her husband, Shiva. Now why would that turn a man on?

Well, from my experience in the seminar, watching men sit up like dominos in reverse showed me men WANT to show up. They WANT to be held to their highest. They want to serve nobly and on some primal level, they want to be there for their queen. One man in the audience said that he knew I wouldn't put up with his shit, and I wouldn't baby him or nag him. I simply cocked my head and said, "Damn straight." He smiled the sexiest, most primal smile. All the men straightened up in their chairs and made this deep groaning sound. Completely wild.

The men shared that they want to know you will "cut off his head" if he strays from his purpose. He wants to know you aren't a pushover. He wants to know you are so devoted to his purpose that you will hold him to the fire no matter what—WITH LOVE. Now here's the important point: if you try to be Kali to keep him on purpose, you may end up being a nagging, judgmental bitch. I've been there, done that. It doesn't work. If you try to be Kali for your own self-confidence, not to be a pushover, to pay your own bills, and take full responsibility for your life, you're on your way in the right direction to feeling your innate power as the Sacred Feminine. Yet, you still won't attract him and you'll still emasculate him.

You must connect with Kali as fierce love. The strength you rely upon to weather the pain of your open heart in the world for the sake of being courageous and savoring every morsel of piercing pain or orgasmic bliss. Kali stands at the gate of your heart and keeps the gate open, reminding you that you can handle anything, you can be fierce love for your beloved, and be open to all that life has to offer. Kali is your strength, she fuels YOUR quest for truth in yourself. She holds YOUR inner masculinity in check, making sure he takes your feminine wisdom, energy, and creativity into the world. When you connect with Kali for the sake of courageously keeping your heart open to experience all that life has to offer, a man knows that you will easily "cut his head off" with a glance if he strays from his purpose, and that you will do so because of your devotional love. He will know that you don't need his approval. You are insatiable for the truth, for what's real in the moment, for the ferocious fullness of life. This makes a man quiver and then show up in his most noble state, humbled and grateful that he met his purpose, being fueled by the deep love of your Kali energy.

WHAT THIS MEANS FOR YOU...

This was an intense three-part lesson:

1. being sexy by having pleasure being alive as a woman,
2. being open hearted for the sake of living ALL of life, and
3. being fierce love, igniting the noble purpose of your beloved.

My recommendation is to re-read this section. First it's awareness and then it becomes a practice.

How can you have pleasure in your body for being alive when you're sleep-deprived?

How can you keep your heart open when asked what you did all day and why you're exhausted? (Argh!)

How do you transform your fury into fierce love when he's making excuses, blaming, and being a victim when you want him to get a job that makes him happy?

This is your practice. Life. And you can do it.

And if you have hit the wall and need support, these situations are the ones where breakthroughs really transform marriages and families. Perhaps our HeartMates Couples Digital Program can support you tremendously, or join our Intimacy Breakthrough Group Coaching program. We turn around lives, and marriages into thriving intimacy. Together. I believe in you sister.

When Mama's Happy Basics

GO EASY ON YOURSELF FROM THE INSIDE OUT

I used to wake up in the morning feeling either this dread for the day or this anxiety to make a difference. I didn't feel that by simply waking up and opening my eyes I was enough. I had to DO something to be enough. Be a better mom. Exercise to lose some weight. Meditate so I wasn't so crabby. Think positive to attract a better life. Make a difference. Be sexier. Be more peaceful. Arrgh! I was afraid if I didn't keep pushing myself to be better, improve, or excel, that my life would fall apart. It was perfectionism at its worse. I learned that I'm already okay. I'm already a good person. I'm already enough. Now I can breathe, appreciate, be grateful, and be in the moment, savoring my son, cherishing my life, shining just because I'm ME. And from that place, take divine action, spirit flowing through YOU as an open vessel of radiance here to serve and illuminate the world.

REVIVING YOUR ENERGY AND YOUR SANITY

Moms, we have to fill our tanks up first so we have something to give our kids and partners. Giving to ourselves first is the most difficult when the to-do list is never-ending and we feel guilty for leaving our little ones. For quick energy boosts, try combining your strolling time with an uplifting guided meditation CD, nap while they are napping even though the laundry won't get done. You'll be a more patient and happy mom when all awaken. Hire the local teenager to fold the laundry or order your groceries online! Have a good cry in the bath once the kids are asleep. Releasing stuck, old energy gives a huge blast of divine energy. Put on some dance tunes and even get on the coffee table with your kids. (Yes, I do that and it's amazing!) Moving our bodies and remembering we're sensual creatures lifts our energy and is a sexy surprise for your partner when he walks through the door!

HOW TO GET OUT OF YOUR HEAD AND INTO YOUR BODY

Our heads are filing cabinets full of wonderful information that we used in the past. Yet when your child needs something, that's happening NOW, not the past. If you allow your mind to spin in circles strategizing to find the answer, your life is passing you by and your child is still crying while your panic sets in with a deeper hold. Understand that all the child is really saying is "Help me understand my pain." We don't need to fix it. Try feeling the moment in your body, not your head. In your body, you are connected to infinite wisdom accessed as a gut feeling, intuition, divine guidance. Breathe, trust the answer is within you, listen and act from feeling. Let your body lead the way and feel the wisdom of the ages course through your veins and the love of the universe in your hands as you pick up your child. Notice empathy leads the way. Divine guidance to meet the needs of your child unfolds, and you remain a vessel for love to work through you, as you. This is a sensual woman.

GETTING GROUNDED AND OPENING YOUR HEART

Getting in your body starts with connecting to the earth. When we're sleep-deprived and trying to control our circumstances, it's difficult to get to that place of calm and peace from where we can make our best decisions. We're more prone to fear, overwhelm, and a closed, protected heart. It's as if we walk on eggshells in a permanent kegel! The quickest way for me to find my power and peace is to imagine that my feet are connected to the earth and I breathe in through my feet, nourishing my body. I breathe in Mother Earth's love, support, and connection. This calms me, relaxes me,

reminds me that I can handle anything. Walk as if your feet are making love to the earth. Notice how this expands your heart with faith, allowing your shoulders to relax, your belly to soften, your forehead to let go, all the while knowing you are a luminous, beautiful, sensual being. From this place affirm that everything is as it's supposed to be and that you are loveable all the time exactly as you are.

THE MORE YOU STOP, THE EASIER MOTHERHOOD BECOMES

It's natural to want to be a perfect mom and avoid mistakes that add up to years of therapy for our kids! The truth, however, is that the more you can stop trying to be perfect, stop feeling guilty for taking time for yourself, stop worrying about how your kids are when you're not with them, stop beating yourself up that you can't get everything done that you used to before the kids, stop holding yourself to a standard that others have for you, the easier motherhood becomes. Motherhood truly becomes an opportunity to love yourself, forgive yourself, and be tender with yourself which translates into a radiant, patient, loving presence for your child and family. People feel safe around you because you're at peace with who you are. The more I stop motivating myself with punishment, guilt, and fear, the more I make room for self-love, divine guidance, and gratitude for the moment. This is when you'll notice kids say the most profound things, because we've made the space for spirit. Now that's the embodiment of a sensual mother— openness to all that is.

Never forget you are not just beautiful, you *are* beauty. You are not just sensual, you *are* sensuality.

You *are* an amazing woman, a gift to your children, your partner, your friends, and community.

You *are* naturally a light in this world without even trying.

Shine fully by taking good care of yourself, taking time for yourself, and being exactly who you are—perfectly imperfect and gloriously delicious YOU!

WHAT THIS MEANS FOR YOU...

Time for some mirror work.

I am going to reread what's above and your delicious job is to look yourself in the mirror every morning and night and say this to yourself until it's your new normal, your new baseline. Mean it, sister. Even if it seems stupid, or makes you cry, or doesn't work for a few nights.. Let it work it's magic.

I am not just beautiful, I am beauty itself. I am not just sensual, I am sensuality itself.

I am an amazing woman, a gift to my children, my partner, my friends, and community.

I am a natural light in this world without even trying. \ I shine fully by taking good care of myself, taking time

for myself.

I love being exactly who I am, perfectly imperfect and gloriously delicious ME!

Powerful Practices for Sumptuous Motherhood

GIVE YOURSELF PERMISSION TO MEET YOUR NEEDS

Where do you get the biggest bang for your buck to fill

your tank? Schedule it NOW and REGULARLY as this is the catalyst for being happy on a consistent basis. Treat this appointment with yourself like you'd treat an important meeting, because it IS! Set an intention for this time to be the space for divine guidance to be revealed. See what magic unfolds.

Allana says: I get my biggest bang for my buck with sitting with a cup of tea or a glass of wine at the end of the day, sunset time, when the sun is so orange and warm on my eyelashes, and I take a breather, say to myself, "Look how far you've come," and I count the ways, feel my connection to Mother Earth... then go make dinner.

DON'T BUY INTO EXCUSES

Excuses like "I need to wait 'til the kids are grown" to be fulfilled. Be creative and find a way to meet your desires now. Want to travel the world? Find the local Little India and begin an adventure today. Our desires are really our yearning for an experience. Sure I want to travel, but really I want the experience of beauty, adventure, love, and joy. And THOSE are available every day, everywhere, in every way.

Allana says: Instead of being disappointed that I haven't manifested my king at the time of this writing, I have decided not to wait until he arrives to have my son inspired by great men. So in his room I have a huge board where we've created this collage called "Great Men with Wise Words." It's a photo of Gabe and everyone from Les Brown to his favorite waiter at Jerry's Deli, then their wisest words for his highest evolution.

START YOUR DAY BEING ENOUGH

Before you even get out of bed, affirm "I am enough."
You need not accomplish supermom deeds to be worthy,

cherished, and accepted. Just being alive you are a gift! You are a shining light of joy, compassion, and heartfelt radiance. It's not "seeing is believing." It's BELIEVING is seeing. Breathe your glorious worth in and out, open your heart and hug that husband, hug those kids, and be grateful for this moment.

Allana says: I remember when my cat Muffin was new to our lives. She's a cuddler. She reminded me not to start the day running. She's luxurious, soft, purring, and because of her Gabe started snuggling with me again in the morning, so I'd start the day saying, "Thank you for this decadence, this beauty, this peace, this deliciousness. I am a vessel for God, already full, unique, and totally taken care of, here to serve and have some fun!"

TEACH KIDS TO RESPECT MOM TIME

My son knew he had to wait until "Seven Zero Zero" to wake me up because I was finding patience and kindness for him. This empowered him to help me while I used my bath time, workout time, and meditation time as sacred "fill me up" time.

Allana says: I swear I couldn't function if I didn't implement this. I mean my sister is a doctor as is her husband, and they have somehow trained their superhuman bodies to survive and thrive on no sleep, yet I am a cranky bitch and need my sleep. I also like that I'm teaching my son boundaries so he knows he has the right to say "No." I even taught him that he has a bucket and when he's cranky it's because his bucket is empty. He is learning what fills up his bucket and will even tell me, "It's time to be quiet. I'm filling his bucket ... Shhhh."

STAY IN THE PRESENT WITH THE KIDS WHEN THEY'RE MELTING DOWN

Don't blame husband/school for their behavior. Don't worry about them being problem kids in the future. It doesn't help the situation. Stay in the moment, heart open, and breathe.

Allana says: Just so you know I'm saying this one because I NEED TO HEAR IT, as I have this awful habit of blaming my son's bad behavior, that looks JUST LIKE HIS DAD'S BEHAVIOR, on his Dad. This one's a biggy for me. I feel like a carwash. I don't think you need to be divorced to feel what I'm feeling. They pick shit up (literally when they're two and figuratively forever). I believe when we can stay present, speak our truth, release blame, and make a request, things go much better and WE feel much better too, having not given away our power to another by overreacting.

LET GO OF YOUR TO-DO LIST

Or finish it and THEN show up fully listening, fully present. Half-present parents create half-present experiences, half-present kids' behavior, and half-present fulfillment for all.

Allana says: I used to have my office smack dab in the middle of the living room. I never stopped working. I had a never ending to-do list and I was always on the computer and was rarely present except at meals. I found that when I moved, created my back bungalow office where I CLOSE the door when I'm done and enter my sanctuary home, first I am way more present with my son, but funny thing, is that I'm still getting my to-do list done, and in a shorter amount of time. I'm also willing to say "NO" to more things that used to go on the to-do list. More present to life seems to be providing more presents. Great moments with Gabe, great men to date, great miracles to bless my life, because now I'm alert and accepting them!

BE WITH NOURISHING FRIENDS

... in a sensual, even naughty way. Eat dark chocolate, go dancing, or draw the drapes and go crazy in the living room, meet under the full moon and dance with the wet grass between your toes, share your journey, enjoy how good it feels to be heard. Fill yourself up then return home telling your man why he's your hero.

Allana says: Two cherished girlfriends are coming over Saturday. After they join me and Gabe for thank you's (all of us on his bed with the nightlight, sharing our lists of gratitude), we'll be doing the usual wine and cheese and chat. In our emails they joked if they should bring lingerie given my newsletter musings, and so I responded "YES!" They will be here three days after the full moon, close enough! We're going to wear our Uggs and lingerie and dance in the backyard celebrating all we have and all that's coming into our lives! Why not!?

RELEASE ENERGY DRAINS

With draining acquaintances and obligations, be kind but firm and say, "I'm honored, yet, no thank you." Your energy is precious and you are always at choice whether to give it away and avoid confrontation, or speak your truth with honesty and kindness and create a life where people honor your time and energy.

Allana says: People literally tell me they want an Allana fix. One of my healing practitioners even told me today that she likes it when I come in as I boost her energy, which is totally wild as I'm there for her to help ME! I say this because we are precious creatures of light and love, and if we aren't being nourished as well, that means we're being drained and we simply don't have time for that anymore. Not if you're committed to being a radiant blessing to the planet. If it's not a "Hell yes!" it's a "Hell no!" and bow out gracefully. Notice what a life of one nourishing event after another does for your confidence and well-being, let alone patience and playfulness with the kids! You MIGHT even have energy for a quickie tonight!!!!

FULFILL YOURSELF NO MATTER WHAT

There is no reason to be envious or jealous of others when your life works. Yet it's easy to have our attention pulled in envy or longing instead of thanking this sister for waking up a dormant part of you. Do what it takes to create the life you love. Be willing to have a life practice of finding fulfillment in the moment so you can be a profound listener, unconditionally loving, and free of judgment with all you meet.

Allana says: I used to be quite jealous of women with great fashion sense, who had their colors done, who looked so damn good! So instead of complaining or being envious, I saved up for this stunning color specialist and also this amazing stylist who helped me create my look in the colors that work for me! Disastrous though, as now I want to go shopping all the time, and I'm still way behind on trends, but I've improved, I feel way more confident, dressing is fun again, and I even get the odd comment of how good I look. Nice!

ADORN YOURSELF TO FEEL LIKE A GODDESS

How would you dress if you were meeting the divine

today? This reminds you that you are a luscious goddess (who happens to drive carpool). Beautiful clothes can put you in the mood, dissolve neediness, and enhance self-confidence. In all your glory and gorgeousness, watch him be attracted to your radiance.

Allana says: I get in moods where I want A LOT of clothes so I go to Forever 21 (even though I'm 50) and H&M and buy a bunch of inexpensive, trendy things that will fall apart by the time they're out of style. I used to do this when I was 35, when I didn't care if they'd get thrown up on or covered in grass stains with my son. Now he's 17 and I'm 50 and we go TOGETHER and get great deals. He tells the truth if I look good or not. Such a doll. Other times I wait and spend a little more on something TO DIE FOR and it becomes one of my signature pieces for years, always making me feel like a queen. The point is that dressing in a way that makes me feel amazing reminds me I'm a piece of ART. I somehow walk taller, I feel more valuable and that always translates into being a more creative, patient, or present mom.

DANCE FOR YOURSELF

Once the kids are at school or in bed, let go of stress, move your hips wider than you normally do, breathe into all tight or anxious areas, forehead, shoulders, stomach, even your "Perma-kegel" (if you're like me). Then dance for him! This way you won't need his attention to feel beautiful which creates the space for him to shower you with attention.

Allana says: I loooooove to dance. I go to my sacred dance class at least three times a month and yet I also do my best to dance when I'm in my head and want to get back in the flow. I prefer music with no lyrics as the words seem to make my mind chatter worse. I love drums. I shake. I feel my feelings. I let it all go and somehow the frustrations and fears of being a mom drain and my wise crone's voice shares her strength and wisdom with me from within. JUST ONE SONG can change the whole day around! I even dance before I have a date to get out of my head and into my body. When I see him I'm not nervous, my breath is full, I'm open and present, sparkling from the inside out.

FEED HIM BY HAND

Being sexy is really about living life sensually, taking time to be present to all your senses. Feed him by hand, choose exotic, savory, exquisite smelling foods or simply make his favorite meal. Also be an example of sensuality by eating a chocolate-covered strawberry in a way that would embarrass his friends. (Watch the cult flick *Dangerous Beauty* again for the asparagus reminder!)

Allana says: I love being more and more aware of my senses while also being more and more courageous to live my true expression moment to moment. As a mom, my son and I created a handmade slip and slide one day after school and I got grass up my ass and had a ball! I believe it was my fourth date with this great guy when I fed him by hand at dinner and it drove him wild. On the one hand he seems to rest into this king energy to be valued and cherished so much, and another part of him got quite primal and sensual with me, so much that when he took me to his home and introduced me to his AMAZING backyard and pool, I stripped naked and went skinny-dipping with glee!

WHAT THIS MEANS FOR YOU...

The point of all these tips is for you to see how small

changes can add up to big results in a mom's life. I like to think of the analogy of water.

Each degree hotter contributes to the boiling point. Who knows when that last action you took is going to tip you into peace! Joy! Bliss! Don't give up!

Take one tip a day, one tip a week, one tip a month. It really doesn't matter, just take baby steps and be consistent.

Over time, life WILL look different, you will feel different, and because you've removed veil after veil covering the real, authentic, grounded happy YOU. Well done, sister. Xox

Eleven Hot Mama Solutions to Get Your Groove On

1. Delegate to Feel More Delicious

It's impossible to be sexy when you're frazzled.

I am hereby giving you permission to ask for help so that your kingdom thrives.

Yes, my queen, I want you to consider shopping for groceries online, and once a week hiring the kid next door to wash and fold your laundry, take out the garbage, and go to the post office for you. Consider hiring a virtual assistant to help you make appointments, research travel, send out your holiday cards. Seriously, how many hours would that buy you a week for YOU to use as sacred time to nourish your sexy soul, sister?

Feel the guilt, and hop in the bath anyway.

Take your journal and ask the question, "How could delegating help me be a sexy, sensual, and satisfied mom?" and see what your higher self answers.

2. Chat with Your Higher Self!

You can't be sexy if there's an elephant in the living room, (unless of course you're draped over its back in a stunning little sequined number!) But seriously, one of the best ways I know to be sexy is to face areas in your life that you are resisting and handle them.

Ahh!!! Scary? Yes, but your sanity is worth it. Sit with yourself and your journal and make room for truth, healing, and transformation in your relationships and life. You may begin this practice sacredly by lighting a candle. Just be sure to ask the questions to your higher self with an open heart and the intention to understand and find healing in your life. Your intention goes a long way.

- "Higher self, tell me something you like about me." (creates affinity)
- "Higher self, tell me something you think we align on." (affirms that you're on the same team)
- "Higher self, tell me something you think I should know." (allows a safe space to tell the truth, the hurt beneath the anger, the pain of not being respected, etc.)

3. It's All About Pleasure!

After a long day of work and mothering, it's important that we make room to nourish ourselves with pleasure. I'm sort of off coffee now and drink "tea-chino." It's my ritual to make a cup and wind down on the porch. Also, one night I was so horny that I wanted to use my vibrator and my batteries had died so I hijacked some from my son's toy. (Please. Haven't you done that?) A girl's got to do what a girl's got to do! Seriously, be willing to self-pleasure with no goal of orgasming. Just be good to your body, enjoy the 8000-nerve-ending clitoris you've been gifted with and watch how it relaxes you, soothes you, and sometimes when you have the energy gets you in the mood to give and receive even MORE pleasure! The point is just because you're tired, doesn't mean you have to forego all pleasure. Try pleasure without a goal and simply enjoy.

4. Face Your Fears and Be Free!

Another way to use your downtime to your advantage is to face your fears instead of getting stuck on email all night.

Kids can tell when mom is preoccupied. You stop being a good listener, you snap at them more, you find fault versus catching them in the act of doing something good. It's a downhill slide and before you know it we're feeling resentful, and all that happened was we didn't take time to listen to our heart, release the stuck feelings, and be tender with ourselves.

If something's bothering you, your energy, confidence, and luscious radiance is at risk, so call that friend, have that cry, talk to a coach, journal until you find clarity. Sexy women are courageous and go to their depths until they find peace and clarity.

5. Teach Kids to Respect MOM Time!

How are we supposed to find our sexy, sensual succulence, and reignite our passions when we're operating on fumes and overwhelm? Healthy boundaries are essential and yet you may have trained your world that you'll always be there for them and if you try to take some time back for you, they give you the guilt trip or complain.

Breathe.

They are addicted to you and your energy! Forgive them for their response and forgive yourself for giving away too much of yourself before you filled yourself up! THEN create a plan for when you need YOU time and present it to the co-workers, boyfriend, husband, children in a way that makes them see that if they become your heroes in supporting you in this, you will be able to gift them with patience, creativity, sensuality, etc.

As I've mentioned, my son knew he had to wait until "Seven Zero Zero" to wake me up because I was finding patience and kindness, *for him*. This empowered him to help ME find it and he felt like my hero while I used the time for a bath, workout, meditation, or simply sleep!

You can explain to your man that, "it would mean a lot to me if / it would make me really happy if you would make dinner tonight so that I could go to yoga and find my juiciness and yumminess for you." Then enjoy your yoga class and be sure to enjoy a sultry night of lovemaking when you get home. In no time at all he'll be asking, "Isn't tonight yoga, honey?" as he remembers to get you out the door on time for class because he's learned how to win!

6. Dance It All Out at Night!

Once my son was in bed, I'd light candles and dance out my frustrations, I'd dance out my tears of being lonely, of yearning for my lover. Sexy women aren't impermeable. Every woman gets scared, angry, and afraid. It's just that sexy women feel, process, and release their feelings so that they're once again tapped into the juicy energy in their body and shining open to the world.

So dance to let go of repressed shame, for connecting with spirit, for turning your man on. I want you to know that as women, it's very effective to let go of stress through movement in our hips for we store so much emotion there. Dance and move your hips wider than you normally do, breathe into all tight or anxious areas including your forehead, shoulders, stomach, vagina. Release self-judgments and commit to love yourself exactly as you are. Dance because you're alive, because you're a woman, a lover. Dance with the intention to get out of your head and back into your body where all your intuition lives. This way you become full from the inside out. This dissolves neediness and attachment, and makes you into an invitation for him to shower you with attention.

7. The Modern Way to Give Roses!

Yes, sexy moms tend to get lots of flowers given to them, yet they don't wait if he forgets. She expresses her self-worth and savoring of beauty with a beautiful bouquet of flowers. Yet it doesn't stop here. After you buy twelve of your favorite flower, write down twelve ways you're a sexy mama, a great lover, a sultry domestic goddess, a succulent wife, an off-the-charts mother, a gorgeous gift to humanity. Create this list and begin a healing ritual and joyous celebration of who you are TODAY. Sit yourself down and read each statement aloud as you put each exquisite stem into the vase, affirming how truly amazing you are.

This may sound corny, yet if you truly take it to heart and begin to offer love versus judgment to yourself, your true confidence and radiance will illuminate your life. Then each time you gaze at the bouquet for the next week or more, you'll be reminded of how sexy and fabulous you are, and as each flower opens and unfolds, you too will be inspired to open into your most luscious self!

8. Get a Hot Mama Dress!

I know that when I'm bloated, I don't feel the slightest bit sexy. Ditto right after my son was born, when I was carrying some extra weight. I had trouble shifting my thinking from "I'm fat" to "I'm voluptuous." I was withholding love to myself instead of giving it. I was turning off my light instead of shining it. I was closed to physical affection instead of open. I was hopeless, believing that I didn't deserve attention instead of welcoming it. When we're down on ourselves, it can be hard to pull ourselves out of a deep, dark hole, so I say get a fabulous dress that looks good no matter what your weight!

Get a dress that makes you feel sexy even if you're still carrying those last ten pounds! Do not wait, I said DO NO WAIT, to be sexy, to love yourself, to own your gorgeousness!

Ladies, we can wait forever. Get a great dress and never again have an excuse for not shining in your radiant sexiness!

9. Bye, Bye Diaper Bag. Hello, Fabulous Purse!

When it comes right down to it, who am I to say that a purse is less spiritual than a priest's outfit? What I really think it comes down to is how you FEEL with it. If a great purse makes you shine from the inside out, makes you feel beautiful, radiant, and luscious, then carry it. If you use the purse from an insecure place to get attention and feel enough, you'll never find a purse good enough to fill that empty hole. So I think it's brilliant if fashion can remind you that you are a light in this world. Take yourself out shopping for a hip new purse. (Especially if you're like me and schlepped a diaper bag around for four years!)

10. Temptress Picnic in the Driveway!

I think it's sexy to plan a picnic for date night once the kids are down. It encourages snuggling, and laying on your side makes the outline of your body so voluptuous and your boobs look great! True or true?

So get a sitter and plan a picnic for a sunset at the beach or at a look-out point. Or if you're saving money, stay in and have a picnic in the driveway in the back of your SUV! Can you imagine how shocked and pleased he'd be if he arrived home to see you all spread out on a big blanket and yummy pillows?

In addition to some delicious food and beverages, bring something you have always dreamed of doing, some vacation catalogs, the calendar of music, sports, events, or festivals in your city and plan some dates in the future. Watch a movie on some device under the stars. Be sure to really savor your time together. Maybe even just listen. We women talk way more than men do. Make space to learn something about him you never knew and watch how he engulfs you in affection and appreciation for a special night.

11. DARK is Good!

Sometimes we're in go-go-go mode and don't feel in the mood to be all feminine when we have laundry to fold, emails to send, and kids to put to bed. The last thing we feel like trying to be is seductive. And yet there's nothing sexier to him than when we're being more masculine than he is! While we WISH our men would grab us and ravish us and take us away from making lunches for kids, sometimes we need to train them. I know it's not fair and not so romantic to have to show him how you want to be claimed, yet I ask you to be DARK so he gets the hint.

Dark with love means keep your heart open, be aware of

your intense love for this man, your primal attraction to him, while letting out your wild side. Once the kids are down, be willing to throw him on the bed and attack him, be willing to pounce on him on the couch putting the remote control down your pants and tell him to find it with his teeth, begin to strip in front of his nighttime zone-out television show, and make out in the living room for a change. Have some fun letting your temptress out and watch how at first you don't think you have the energy, but once you get started, you feel energized and gorgeous. Watch how he'll surprise you the next time.

LIFE-SAVING PRACTICES FOR THE EMPOWERED MOTHER

Imagine as you're reading this, you're close to me. Notice how I appear bitchy, know-it-all, and cold. You may even feel tired or perhaps pissed off and dominated by me.

Now open to me as you read this and notice how I appear warm, helpful, loving. You may feel my love for you, my belief in you. The wisdom might shift things internally and make you feel empowered. Yet the only thing that changed is YOU!

Now let's take this into your life. Imagine being close with someone you're sitting beside at a meeting or on a park bench, then imagine being open to the universe having it's way with your connection at that moment.

Close your eyes and imagine making love when you are closed, then open. How about when talking to your children. Closed or open?

How about when seeing your body in the mirror? Close to your body and watch the judgmental words begin to cut away at your self-worth, only noticing what's wrong. Then imagine opening to yourself as you witness your divine vessel in front of the mirror. Notice how you are radiant, beautiful, a goddess, gorgeous, perhaps even moving yourself to tears in humble gratitude for the miracle that is you.

Sexy women, hot mamas, and beneficial women on the planet are those who choose to open. They seem inviting and magnetically attractive because they are a YES to who they are.

ASKING FOR HELP

Picture this: You are all drained up, squelched, empty, feeling needy, overwhelmed, panicked, feeling out of place, unworthy.

Got it? Hang in there I won't keep you here for long, but don't we all feel that way sometimes?

Now imagine how it would feel, coming from this empty, needy place, to ask for help.

Your voice is atrocious, all constricted, people look at you like you're weak, you feel like a burden, you want to give up and just hide. Pretty awful, huh?

This is a place where our feelings of aloneness create that very circumstance on the outside. People are actually unable to step up and help because we're pushing them away with our neediness and our hands aren't open to receive; they're clinging and grasping.

Now shake that off, sister! Hands up in a circle from below out wide to above your head, then bring them down the center of your body, closing your hands as you move them downward, cleansing any negative energy you found and shooting it straight down into the earth. Whoosh!

Okay. Better?

Now I want you to imagine that you are dressed in a regal gown. You are taken by the most handsome knight to your glorious throne and you take a seat. You look and feel like a queen. You rest. Open. Back tall. Heart open. Slight smile.

Warmth for your disciples and appreciation for your support staff. With humble reverence for your position, you feel the grand yet joyous responsibility to the whole kingdom.

You are feeling the overflowing abundance of your thriving kingdom, you easily give freedom of choice to all knowing you have plenty of help, and then ask for help. Notice how you feel empowered and open. Notice how safe and attractive you are to people when you give them a choice to help or not. Notice how inviting you are to others and how they'd be honored to help. Feel how your kingdom flourishes because you've delegated.

Pretty powerful, huh?

ENTER THE CHAMBERS OF YOUR HEART AND BEYOND

Imagine you've cut off your body and you are just a head. Imagine racing through your to-do list, feeling there isn't enough time, concerned about how things will turn out, doing your best to be tightly in control, strategizing, manipulating situations, keeping to your agenda, single-focused, and not open to support and feeling alone and overwhelmed. The more you think about it, the worse your head feels, so constricted, contracted, controlling, and stressed out.

How many of us have days like that? Ahhhh. So take a few deep breaths and now imagine you are no longer a head. You are a body. Drop down through your neck, relax your shoulders, and move into your heart cavity. Open it, widen it, deepen it, and press it toward your rib cage, with full breath taking up space. Breathe life into every chamber, bring light to the darker chambers, breathe compassion, understanding, validation, and honoring into every chamber and notice that you experience a deeper quality of rest, enough-ness, relaxation, trust, and faith.

Feel how huge and vast your heart is. Now move lower past your heart, past your relaxed stomach, into your pelvis, your womb, your vagina.

Now I know this may sound weird, but stay with me.

Imagine your yoni (the most sacred, reverent word for our glorious vulva) open and connected into Mother Earth. Feel safe, surrendered, and sinking down into Mother Earth's energy, letting her fill you with every breath. Mother Earth and now YOU are as wide as a forest, as deep as the ocean, as fierce as a tornado, as calm as a gentle breeze blowing through a field of wheat at sunset. See if you can let go soooo much and feel Mother Earth's power in you sooooooo much that you feel as if you ARE everything, intuition itself. Notice if you feel so powerful that you can let down your guard and feel calm, grounded, empowered, full. When a woman is not spinning and she is grounded in this energy, it almost looks as if she's just had an orgasm, so magnetically attractive and sensual.

Honestly, this is a great exercise to do in the car while waiting to pick up the kids, you will be listened to on the first try, truly! It's great to do in the shower after a long day before you go to bed. You will be the space to be honored, adored, and cherished for you know your worth.

THE PERMA-KEGEL

This exercise is a fun one, (I think.)

Next time you're at a meeting or parent night or even a night out with the gals for a kick, stand up, tighten your jaw, your shoulders, cave your chest, tighten your stomach, and clench your kegel (vagina). Then introduce yourself or say "hi" to someone. Then try to smile or relax. It doesn't work! You look like you have a pickle up your butt and you'll turn people off! And yet how many times, if we REALLY checked in, are we walking around trying to be safe as we walk on eggshells contracted from head to kegel!?

While it sounds funny, I was like this for decades. I remember the day so vividly when I was five years old, dancing in the living room to the "Jesus Christ Superstar" album, running so fast around the ottoman that I was almost horizontal with the floor, screaming with delight, when WHAM! My dad punched a hole through the wall. I remember being terrified that it could have been my head. The look on his face sent shivers up my spine. I don't think I let go of my Perma-kegel since then. I literally was three steps ahead of anyone, such a huge people pleaser, anything to make sure I was safe and would never be scared like that again.

Now back to this present moment, my sweet sister, I ask you to relax each part of your body I mentioned above. Your shoulders, heart, stomach, hips, pelvis until your vagina is open, fully. Imagining your heart and brain and lungs all reside in your wise pelvis, like there's a circle of ancestors, wise crones, glorious goddesses in there all gathered on your behalf, providing you with spot-on intuition and instinct and responses aligned with your highest good. Noticing yes, that our pelvis IS our sexual center, yet it's also our creative center. Notice the phrase "gut feeling" and take it a little lower. Yes, your deepest pelvis has a glorious sense of intuition. I believe this is where our connection to the divine resides as a woman. And so, at that meeting, parent council gathering, night out with the girls, or the next time you speak to your kids or hubby, introduce yourself as if speaking through your pelvis, with this energy flowing, relaxed and totally yourself. Worlds apart, yes? Confident, sexy, calm, creative, and peaceful women are juicy from the inside out.

. . .

BRINGING HOME YOUR LITTLE GIRL

Make some time to be alone for this practice as it can be very moving. I may need to make a recording for this as it's difficult to read and get into it, yet I want to give you everything I have!

When a woman is sad and stays in the victim cycle, unable to forgive herself, this practice is very helpful.

Take a few deep breaths, letting go of the day, sinking deeper and deeper, more and more relaxed with each exhale. Find the area in your body where you are most constricted when you get scared, sad, or angry. Breathe into this place. No need to fix or change, just BE with it. Even welcome it if you can.

Imagine your higher self and I become very, very small and travel into your body where this contracted area is … perhaps your heart, your stomach, your throat. Smaller and smaller, darker and darker until we see the core of this contracted energy, and there's a little short door, it's open and we go inside. After our eyes adjust, we find two little chairs and sit down. Across the room you, your higher self and me, we are looking at the scared little girl part of yourself.

The little girl is in black and white with her back turned to you. Let your higher self talk to her, ask her for forgiveness for abandoning her, ignoring her. Tell her you see her, understand her, and will always protect her from now on. Imagine sending a stream of love from your higher self heart to the little girl. As you do, see her turn from black and white to color. Turn around and look at you and your higher self smiles and opens her arms and the little girl runs into them and you hold her there, welcoming her home, holding her, rocking her, resting in this union, allowing tears to heal everything, committing to listen to her and honoring her.

Until we listen to and validate this little girl, she won't heal.

She's in front of our sexiness and we show up as needy or controlling to men. Once healed, she has great wisdom, discernment, insight, intuition, and instinct to share, not to mention fabulous freedom of expression and playfulness to delight our day.

LETTING GO OF POISON—ANGER RELEASE

Unexpressed anger stuck inside poisons us and dissolves our playfulness, patience, presence, and pleasure as a mother. Journaling out your truth, then reading it daily over several days, then burning it is very effective. Hitting pillows and screaming obscenities in front of the family would freak them out of course, yet see if you can find a time when you are alone and go for it.

Getting rid of stuck anger in the body and mind is very cathartic and amazing for giving women a sexy glow of authentic radiance from within.

If you have a willing victim (girlfriend), something quite effective is going into a full-on tantrum together. Being witnessed, heard, and gotten while getting her. Stamp your feet, yell obscenities or jibberish, whine and moan, shake out your bodies. It feels amazing and eventually ridiculous and you will both feel worlds better.

These exercises might seem over the top, bizarre, and you may find yourself saying you don't have the time, or you'd never do that. Which of course is just fine! Just be sure you really own your choice to be right or be happy. Being right often means we keep anger (poison) in our bodies, eating away at our own soul while we give away our power, stewing over the past. The choice to be happy means you let something go in mind and in body that may not be fair at all, for the sake of your own happiness, and becoming present to the magic of the moment. Radiant moms are sexy moms.

TELL THE TRUTH ABOUT FEELING HOPELESSNESS, BEING A VICTIM

After my divorce, I stayed in my house, looked good, lived the illusion of safety, beat myself up that I needed to work harder, shared nothing of my situation, and pretended I was fine, wasn't willing to sell and downsize, was looking for man to save me, an investment to save me, communicated from a closed heart, disconnected from my intuition, picked a wrong guy to date who I knew wouldn't support me so I could be right that I wasn't enough, and in the end I'd be left, when he did leave. I had to feel the real panic I'd been living with, panic about money, about security, about safety, about God. Panic since Dad hit hole in wall when I was little.

When we become victims, we're only doing this because keeping our heart open hurts too much. We're resisting feeling. It's our way of numbing out, being in denial, avoiding taking responsibility for our lives. It causes depression, neediness, and cloudiness to make important decisions. I know my heart is closed when something good happens and I feel a sense of addictive relief, I'm saved!!!! Relief is when you think something on the outside can make you feel enough on the inside, and yet it's the surest way to give your power away. There's nothing to feel relief about when your heart is open, all is well, and you're taking 100% responsibility for creating your life.

Notice how I felt better in the house? Am I my house? Is my worth my house?

Notice how I felt better dating a man and then crushed when he left? Yet, am I my relationship?

Notice how I was willing to give away my peace, power,

and sanity to a man's opinion, to be his slave for attention—it was even more painful to admit—and yet liberating to own and shift.

ONCE WE DO THIS FOR OURSELVES, WE CAN TEACH THIS LEVEL OF AUTHENTIC MATURITY TO OUR KIDS!

I shifted by opening my heart, feeling my feelings, and telling the truth. The only way through is through. This shift also includes forgiveness of self, others, the situation. It's about being at peace with emotions, feeling them layer after layer until we see what belief is driving them, shifting that belief if it's outdated so as to reconnect to your purpose, and be a willing vessel to flow with passion and inspiration from source.

For example, when I was angry that we'd be late for school and I pushed or manipulated my son to get him ready, he sensed my game, dug in his heels, and consciously or subconsciously took away my power. When I relaxed and told the truth, that I was really scared to be late, to look bad, to be a bad mom, that he'd miss something important and not have a happy future—pure raw me, nothing to hide, here were my fears—I simply asked him to tell mommy what I could do to be a better mom, to get us to school on time. He became completely cooperative and delighted to help me.

I swear that being open and surrendered IS the most powerful way to be. Yet it's so counter-intuitive. Pushing seems stronger, we're more in control, and yet I believe openness is the most effective choice to dissolve victim frustrated energy as a mom.

I Just Don't Want to Have Sex!
(OR AT LEAST NOT WITH YOU)

Are you an exhausted mom who works and pretends to be asleep to avoid having sex when he comes to bed? Has the financial stress of the economy extinguished the flame of passion in the bedroom, making him all prickly, edgy, and grumpy to be with? Are you having unsatisfying sex? Obligatory sex? No sex? Feeling resigned, lonely, or hopeless? Are you so powerful, beautiful, and confident sexually that your husband shies away from taking you the way you crave to be taken? Do you love how successful you are professionally, yet yearn to be ravished to your core physically?

Here's the truth. You can be ravished to the core. You are the power in the relationship. You are in the lead. You are the juice, the spark, the creative force. You can have anything you want.

What's in the way? Validated anger? Justified blame? Betrayal? Unfairness? Even feeling timid to really set yourself free? Hopelessness that if you do, you might be rejected?

I get it.

Yet, it's our job to feel, process, and release these validated, understandable emotions.

They indeed are telling you something isn't working. Yet holding onto them guarantees things will KEEP not working and get worse.

Remember, when you're running on empty, acting out of obligations, not nourishing yourself, suffering through unsatisfying connections on all levels, being overly prideful by not asking for help, allowing elephants in the living room to outnumber members of the household, then you're in trouble.

It's time for us to get over the guilt by telling the truth. Guilt is unexpressed anger. What are you angry about and deal with in a healthy manner? Then fill up your tank first, take care of your well-being, sleep, exercise, take baths, listen to sensual, groovy music on a walk in nature, SHAVE. For goodness sake, my luscious sister, give yourself permission for pleasure for even two minutes by drinking in the sunset, letting the breeze flirt with your hair, pet the cat for two minutes straight, have a tickle fight before you make the bed, buy that decadent body oil and take two extra minutes to slather your gorgeous body temple, because when mama's happy, everybody's happy.

Seriously, it's that simple, yet not that easy because it's habitual and somehow addictive to stay mad, have something to complain about. Staying angry feeds the anger. Letting go means a part of your identity dies and it feels like a death. It withdraws, shakes, desires to eat a bag of chips, the unexpected tears or crankiness. Keep breathing. You'll make it.

As the life coach to Leeza Gibbons, an expert for eHarmony, and a coach for many women and couples, I can tell you that when we women start withholding sex, we're shooting ourselves in the foot, pushing away the very connection we yearn for. He's been a shit and I get it. So what REALLY needs to happen is communication that allows for truth, forgiveness, and solutions.

Solution: Create a sacred time to talk, perhaps thirty minutes, where each person is only allowed to say "thank you" to the other person's share. This makes it safe to tell the truth, no interrupting or judging allowed. Then you ask three simple but profound questions back and forth, and practice impeccable listening:

> Tell me something you like about me. (back and forth about five minutes)
> Tell me something you think we align on. (the same as above)

Tell me something you think I should know about our sex life. (until thirty to forty minutes is complete on the timer)

If you really have the intention of healing, of listening, of sharing without blame, you'll be amazed at the depth of what is profoundly revealed. Then you never speak about what the other said in the communication exercise, yet take action in the direction of healing and rejuvenating your relationship.

As your sexual relationship improves, you can let this communication exercise get sexy, sensual, and steamy if you want to turn him on:

Tell me something that turns you on.
Tell me something you love about oral sex.
Tell me a fantasy you'd like me to know about. Tell me a way you like to be pleasured.
Tell me what you love about our bodies, hearts and souls together.

As a private, exclusive coach to clients around the world, I can tell you that financial stress and the lack of clear delegation of duties is the number one reason relationships fall apart, followed by the loss of a child which either tears them apart or binds them together. Remember, financial stress can ALSO bring a couple together when the woman knows what to say to the man.

Solution: He needs to know that you—no matter what happens to his job, the money, his status, his ability to provide the way he has—love him and you're not leaving. (Of course if there is a gambling problem or similar addiction, that is different.) He needs to know that even if you're scared, in doubt, embarrassed, unsure, or uncomfortable, that you will keep your heart open to him, love him, and stand by his side. He needs to know that while you respect and admire his business savvy, that you love him, the man. You are there to offer your powerful intuition for a creative, resourceful solution while offering your light, radiance, and belief in him to get through this.

Do this and men relax, open up, reconnect. and feel safe to be intimate again.

As a family and relationship expert with expertise in sexuality and intimacy, I have inspired relationships from no sex for two years to quickies every Tuesday at lunch, from the stone cold silent treatment to connected candle-lit dinners, from predictable sex while doing the grocery list in her head to swinging from the chandeliers. (Well, actually it was a ropes course they did together, then made mad, passionate love having regained trust for one another!)

Again, nine times out of ten, the woman giving herself permission to feel her emotions, permission to express her truth, permission to fill herself up with pleasure, and from fullness design the life she wanted... this process creates the breakthrough.

Solution: I've had the humble pleasure of helping to transform women from frumpy to sexy, ashamed to orgasmic, running on fumes to exploding with energy, joy, and pleasure. In my Heartmates For Her digital program we focus on redefining flirting, engaging in pleasure, becoming at peace in our bodies NOW, not after we lose ten pounds, being sisterly instead of competitive with women, exploring feminine power versus masculine power at work and at home, sensual dance movement practices, true forgiveness, learning how to visit our darkness and express fierce love vs. nagging, learning to be playful, even goofy, being REAL, authentic, radiant, and at peace with who we are.

Remember, sensuality and spirituality are one.

Sexuality is sacred. Pleasure is healing. Your bodies are good, true, and beautiful. When you're overflowing and full of confidence, love, and joy, it ripples into your relationships, family, and career. And when you don't, it can be a living hell for you and all you love.

So I work on remembering that while I am still challenged and growing. I'm grateful to be alive and savoring the moments the best I can. I love the part of me that gets scared, feels ashamed or afraid as I would my own child who is asking for a hug. Somehow that softens things and I can move forward with compassion and commitment again.

I say "no" to things and people that take me away from pleasure, that drain my energy, that don't honor me. Sometimes I know right away, sometimes it takes me a while. I notice that when I'm blaming or being competitive, or a victim, something's off. I check in if it's me and I shift. If it's them or a situation, I gracefully decline and complete.

I've decided that everything can be done with pleasure, if not gratitude. Acts of pleasure make me feel good, juicy, luscious, and radiant. I dance, have baths, walks in the woods, wear my favorite clothes, light candles even at my computer, wear heels as I unload the dishwasher if it's the ONLY way I can figure out to do it with pleasure! I make believe I'm giving donations when paying bills or at least say "thank you, thank you, thank you" for my lights, gas, car, home, garbage man, health care, etc. to stay in pleasure! Pleasure is a choice, what do you choose beautiful?

Five Effective Tools That Strengthen Relationships

1. The Dyad: Two-Way Communication

I mentioned this above in connecting more deeply with your higher self, in creating a bridge when needing to talk about sexuality, and I also recommend this on a regular, ongoing basis to keep communications healthy.

Men cringe when we say, "I need to talk," yes?

What if you completely shifted the paradigm and "talking" was a weekly delicious, safe, intimate, vulnerable, and nourishing time to connect?

What if you always wore something nice, smelled good, smiled, praised him in thanks for making this special time together, and honored each other with safe, unconditionally loving answers of "thank you?"

I learned this from Satyen and Suzanne Raja of Warrior Sage.

> "Tell me something you like about me." (creates affinity)
> "Tell me something you think we align on." (reminds you that you're on the same team)
> "Tell me something you think I should know." (allows a safe space to tell the truth, the hurt beneath the anger, the pain of not being respected, etc.)

Sometimes specific issues are really on your mind and you need a safe, productive way to bring it up for resolution:

> "Tell me something you think I don't understand."
> "Tell me something you would like help with." "Tell me something you yearn for."

"Tell me something you are afraid to tell me."
"Tell me something you want me to know from your deepest heart."
"Tell me something that makes you sad (angry, betrayed, hopeless, scared, alone)."
"Tell me something you want to create in your life (our family, our relationship, our future)."

2. Guy Time

Ladies, don't you agree that our men need to be with other great men you respect on a regular basis?

As amazing as we are as women, nothing we do can replace how great it is for him to be with men he respects, men who challenge him, men who insist he stay true to his purpose.

Inspire him to be vigilant and no longer hang out with men who complain, whose lives are falling apart, who are resigned or negative. Instead encourage him to spend weekly time, preferably outdoors, with male friends or mentors you respect so he can let go, relax, laugh, and be real.

Also my friends, if you're glad to have him out of your hair and enjoy a night to yourself, great!! If not, and have any feelings of abandonment, rejection, loneliness, or not enough'ness when he leaves, don't blame these feelings on him. This is your own personal quiet time to reflect on why your heart is closing, why you're questioning your worth, or why you're feeling scared. Take this time so that you can feel the feelings you have been repressing, let them surface with compassion for yourself. Let them dissolve and fill that void with self-love, self-care, and potentially some divine action. Notice that if you keep this practice up, neediness will have dissolved and full, heartfelt yearning for your beloved will flood your open heart when he walks through the door.

3. Girl Time

I believe nothing in this world can replace a great group of women; women that hear you, see you, love you, and will tell you the truth. Let go of any time spent with women who gossip, man bash, compete, or complain. Life is too short to spend your precious downtime with people that bring you down. Check in after a phone call, a cup of coffee, a quickie to the mall, or a full girls' night out.

Are you depleted or nourished? Did you feel heard?

Did you relax to your core and not have to work to get a word in?

Did you feel reminded of your worth for being exactly who you are?

Spend regular time with goddesses who remind you of your worth. And how does your man react when you say you want to go out with the girls? If he's glad to have you out with the gals and knows that you'll come home more radiant than when you left, you are a lucky woman. If you notice that he feels neglected, jealous, or left behind, don't let him blame these feelings on you. With compassion, understanding, and assurance, encourage him to use this time to reflect on why he finds it challenging to support you supporting yourself. Does it make him feel abandoned, not needed, unimportant? See if he thinks giving to yourself is somehow taking away from giving to him? Have you taken such good care of him that he's timid to learn to fix supper for himself? Has your mothering with the kids made him feel inadequate putting them to bed? Tell him you believe in him and encourage him to use this time to get closer to the kids. You breathe and leave, cry in the car if you have to, then go out and have some nourishing fun.

4. The Modern Way to Dance for Him

I know you've probably heard about all the pole dancing classes women are taking. I remember back when I surprised my first husband with a sexy little dance whilst he was working from home and he shunned me away saying he was too busy. Second husband got all nervous and fidgety when I would strip for him, and who's the only thing these two have in common here?

Me. Ouch.

Was I uncomfortable with my sexuality, and projecting it onto them? Had my shame or timid nature around expressing the real me attracted men who I subconsciously KNEW wouldn't accept me so that I could be right that I was defective?

I took a pole dancing class and was in tears by the second class. I could open and express myself in a small box and any sexual and sensual expression outside of that made me terrified, feel ashamed, afraid of being rejected, and afraid to be judged. I learned that I was attracting men that were uncomfortable with their sexuality just like me! So I moved through it and WOW! My last long-term boyfriend LOVED me dancing for him and what was great was that I actually enjoyed it, too! I learned to love my body, my expression, my coyness, my inner nasty girl, as well as my goddess, my queen, my Sacred Feminine spirit. GO FOR IT! First dance for YOU and come to peace with exactly who you are. Turn yourself on! Perfectly imperfect. Whole and complete. You!

I love my workshops with women where we dance all the feminine archetypes for one another, celebrating where they're confident, masterfully bringing forth the flavor of the feminine they're not certain about, watching her EMBODY this new capacity and soar. It truly moves me to tears. We women are magnificent.

And then of course they gift this magnificence and dance for their partners.

Transformation. Bliss. Freedom.

The Sacred Feminine embodied as a sexy mom.

5. 100% Responsibility for Your Life

I wish, I wish, I wish it were different, yet the bottom line in every situation that pisses you off is that the other person is triggering something in you.

If someone says you're a bad cook and you know you're a total gourmet, you kind of look at them with disbelief yet it doesn't hurt your feelings. Yet, if someone says you're not doing enough and you know that you're stretched to the limit and you're operating on fumes, you blow your top! Gotcha! Know that if anything pushes your buttons, there is a shred of truth in what they say and it's your job to dismiss yourself and forgive them because they've only cast a light on an unresolved issue.

Then be kind to yourself.

You've done your best and now you've found some avoidance, denial, righteousness, or feel like a victim. This is a new moment that you can take 100% credit for: own it, acknowledge it without self-judgment, forgive yourself, and extend love to this part of you that is most likely scared, sad, or angry.

See what feelings come up to be released, again, *without judgment*. There is always wisdom on the other side of resistance. Let go, feel, forgive, accept what is ... insights, new choices, new boundaries, new experiences. Wisdom is at hand.

And what's great is that your new found strength, insight, power, and peace has been inside you all along, ready to be birthed. You may come to a place where you can even thank the other person for bringing this to your attention.

To me, that's the modern relationship. A sacred partnership meant to ignite the highest in each other. And being so self-responsible and free of blaming that as we grow, we hold unconditionally loving space for the other to evolve and celebrate the journey together through time.

Part 4: The Babe is Single?

No-Nonsense Dating Tips for Single Parents

(From Allana on Fox KUSI 9 San Diego)

I used to sense there would be a time when I would be on television more. Now it's a reality. I used to think that it was my ego, trying to be enough, and yet now I've surrendered. I simply love loving people, inspiring them, giving of my energy and enthusiasm. I can feel the timing and cooperation of camera people, lights, sound, directors, talent, audience members, like a well-oiled machine operating in unison to serve the greater good. Turns me on.

I remember, for CBS 3 in Philadelphia, I was in the makeup room with Joe Piscopo shooting the shit about relationships and his upcoming show in Atlantic City. I am grateful that I'm courageous enough to give myself permission to do what I really love to do. I love to answer questions with passion, vulnerability, and the wisdom I've gained over time to serve another. Rocks my world. Give yourself permission to do what YOU love. For me it's as if the whole universe has its way with me when I let go and be me!

So here are some dating tips from a segment I did a while back. I would love to hear back from any of you single moms about what works and doesn't work with dating!

1. Before going on out on a date, look in the mirror and say to yourself, "I didn't fail. I am simply more deeply committed to ME. I am open to a man who sees, honors, and celebrates me."
2. Don't bring men around your kids until you're exclusively dating and don't exclusively date until you've brought them around your best friends. Enjoy the process!
3. Once in an exclusive relationship, consider deeply your children's opinion of your partner. Often we are unconscious to old, sabotaging patterns and attract a new flavor of your ex. See if your kids shine brighter around them or not.
4. Tell the truth when dating. Are you looking to remarry, looking for life companionship, looking for a casual partner for sex, social events, travel? Don't play games or waste their time or yours.
5. If you mess up, apologize immediately. "I'm sorry, I made a mistake. How do I make it right?" Vulnerability and confidence are very sexy.
6. This should not need to be said, but have safe sex. Both parties carry condoms and use them. Period.
7. Women, decide ahead of time your truth about who pays. Traditional or Dutch, be clear, consistent, and grateful.

Single Mom Perspective

Be clear that you're amazing on your OWN first. Then don't look to him to save you, make you feel safe, or pay your bills. Do your inner work until you know you are a capable, intelligent woman who finds safety and confidence from inside your heart, not from a man.

WHAT THIS MEANS FOR YOU...

If you're a single mom, or supporting a friend who's a single mom, where are you being yourself and where are you compromising? Where are you speaking and where are you withholding your truth? Are you coming from fullness or emptiness on your dates? Journal here about the truth of your journey. If you have a single friend, I never encourage giving unsolicited advice, yet when and if she asks, if you're taken some time to really listen, you'll be able to steer her in the highest direction.

Single Moms Creating Sparks of Passion

"I want to see you. Tomorrow. Morning." I was short of breath. Men just didn't claim me like this in life. They seem wishy washy asking what would I like to do, where would I like to go. I have to decide enough as a single working mom. I yearn for a man who knows what he wants. And man, oh man, was I happy when this new man I was dating wanted me!

And yet I remembered the days as I was learning how to NOT be so needy, trying to find my independence, and choosing to open my own doors. I had been pissed if a man told me what to do. Back then I'd loved knowing I could provide for myself, think for myself, even orgasm for myself (handy little "rabbit", yes girls? Ha). It felt sooo much better than going to Trader Joe's and wondering, "Is that him? Is that him?" to every unsuspecting male passerby. And yet it attracted surfers, and new age feminine men.

Later on, thank the universe, I got to a place where sparks of passion were flying indeed!!!

I've learned that I needed to expand into a deeper, grounded, luscious, feminine place. It's certainly NOT a softening of my power, yet it is a relaxing of my over-developed masculine side and inviting my powerful feminine side to step up.

Moms, haven't you ever fantasized that our boyfriends or husbands would walk right into the room, slowly yet straight for us, eyes fixed on us, grab us by the small of our back, and stand close to us with a deep even breath. We want them to NOT move their shoulders or head one bit, just keep them fixed on us yet sway US ever so gently with their hips and try something like, "Get dressed. I'm taking you out." ESPECIALLY if he's never talked to us like this. And we want them to do this with a heart open, a sly twinkle in their eye, as if devouring us with their consciousness. And of course he has to be present or it will seem fake or even condescending and we'll probably slap him, right?

Pregnant moms, be willing to invite him to claim you by taking a few moments to breathe before he comes home, light some incense, put on some music, change your clothes, move your hips a bit. Even five minutes of this will totally change your energy before he comes home. Or if you're coming home last, tell him it would mean a lot to you if you could have ten minutes to yourself and then shower him with your luscious radiance when you reappear.

With kids it's more challenging to get into your feminine because you're taking care of them all the time. Yet begin a ritual of TV OFF before dinner, music on, candles lit, and mom changes into something more comfortable. And even if it makes the kids puke, kiss him for at least six seconds and breathe into your vagina as you do so. Ground your body and show the kids what true love, honor, and adoration looks like. Watch how that puts him in the mood to be far more receptive to your request to clear the table and put the kids down while you get ready in the bath for a delicious night.

And if you're a single mom, STILL do all these rituals and hug your kids and dance with them on the coffee table. Sparks of passion can be sexual or sensual. Sensual is when you are savoring life's juiciness until you feel overflowing. Sexual is when you put new batteries in your vibrator like I do and enjoy your body regardless! This is how to feel full, ripe, peaceful, and divine! This is our birthright, sisters!

WHAT THIS MEANS FOR YOU...

Single or married, being a delicious invitation for your man to claim you is a practice. So often we just stay in our masculine do-do-doing and make no room for them to claim us. I invite you to take real action steps before a date or before your man comes home to turn back into the luscious woman you are.

This isn't weak. It's strong, for you have to surrender, open, slow down, trust, and believe you are worth it.

You know your flavor of feminine.

Be her and watch the night unfold much differently than usual. XOXOXO.

Guilt: This Single Mother's Middle Name

My mind wouldn't shut off.

"Allana, if you take time for yourself, aren't you afraid you'll seem selfish? How dare you fill up your tank when there's laundry, bills, and dishes left to do! If you take time for you, you'll let down your family! If you don't get everything done, your life will become chaos, fall apart, and you'll look like an idiot! If you regain your sensuality and radiance from within and become the sexiest creature your friends' husbands have ever seen, aren't you afraid you'll threaten your friends or worse, lose them?"

I was afraid of all these things and more. In fact, I still am afraid, but I've decided to be sexy, sensual, and satisfied anyways.

When I realized I was pregnant the week after my mom died, all at once I was angry, sad, and elated. My marriage was rocky and we were renovating the house. I remember giving birth on my side, clinging to my girlfriend, my back to my husband. He quit his job the next day. I lost it. I would cry and scream hysterically, then put on a happy face with friends. I was sleep deprived, overwhelmed, and had lost all faith. One day I looked into my newborn's eyes and felt like a failure. He looked back with unconditional love, as if to remind me that deep inside there was a joyful, peaceful mom to inspire him. That day I stopped living the lie. I ended my marriage.

Single motherhood triggered many fears and I battled old victim patterns of wanting to be saved, of not trusting men, of being addicted to people pleasing, or being a controlling bitch to get my way. I had trouble finding my sanity let alone thirty-six minutes for a pedicure. No one taught me that I am a precious ecosystem that needs nurturing. No one taught me to feel feelings and let them guide me versus indulge in them and be a drama queen. No one taught me how to surrender and trust my intuition, trust the universe, spirit, angels guiding my every move. No one taught me that guilt is a manufactured emotion! Just like worry! It's not real! It's a lame excuse (destructive, as well) to not have the courage to feel my anger, or take healthy appropriate action in alignment with my truth.

Letting go of the guilt felt like jumping off a cliff into the unknown as I learned by trial and error how to have boundaries, how to create time for me, how to quiet my spinning mind. Slowly I began to re-discover my girlfriends, my fashion, my faith, my dreams, my peace. I forgave myself and made amends with the father. I took sacred dance movement and erotic dance classes, I performed the Dangerous Beauty monologue in an acting class, I went to church, and signed up for Match.com. Like a seed that is growing but we can't see it until it peaks through the soil, one day I woke up and all of a sudden I trusted the universe. I felt beautiful again, but from the inside out.

I played Slip n' Slide in the back yard with my son. Can you say grass up the ass? Ha! We still danced on the coffee table. But I also had I the energy, openness, and confidence to be ravished by my man. I didn't feel envy or competition with other women anymore because I loved myself for exactly who I was right at that moment. When I felt guilt I knew it was an invitation to feel more deeply, honor my truth more fully, step more authentically into my power. What a journey. I learned that there's really nowhere to go but back home to myself. There's really nothing to do but be me.

Listen. Surrender. All is well. Life is good. And so it is.

WHAT THIS MEANS FOR YOU...

I'm not a PhD with a lot of letters behind my name. I'm

just a regular gal who speaks her mind (Ha!). I do believe that things like sadness, anger, joy, and gratitude are authentic feelings with messages for us to listen to for our highest good.

Thus, do the best you can to recognize if you are experiencing something "surface", like guilt or worry.

Take a moment and feel what's beneath that.

Feel what you don't want to feel, like the true fear or anger or sadness.

Now THAT we can work with, feel, validate, listen to, and ultimately shift.

Get out your journal right now and begin talking with your emotions and ask what they want to tell you.

Mother's Day For the Single Mom

Feeling Sexy or Sad? Truth? Some days I was thrilled I didn't have to make nicey-nicey and co-parent with my son's dad. It was great running the ship according to MY rules. On other days I was exhausted and yearned for someone else to tag team with. Take the garbage out, a shoulder to lean on, for a warm body to hold me, to make love with!

Mother's Day makes it all the more obvious that I'm a single, motherless mom. Not the way I thought it would all turn out playing Barbies growing up. And yet here I am and here are so many moms these days. As a coach to amazing women around the world, and as an expert to single moms for dating sites and business organizations, I'm often asked, "How do we be and stay sexy as mothers when we're exhausted, lonely, and frustrated?"

I liken it to Mother Earth. She has tornadoes, earthquakes, and thunder storms. And she has clear lakes of glass, warm breezes through fields of flowers, sunsets that warm your face.

Being sexy as a mother is about being at peace with ALL

the weather. We moms lose our sensuality when we resist the flowing life that's trying to have its way with us and support our evolution and guide us safely along our path. So flow sisters! Feel your feelings, embrace them all, and love them. Embrace life when you're cranky and love that part of you! Embrace life when you're horny and take the batteries out of the kids' toys like I did (Ha!) and pleasure yourself once they're in bed! Emotions pass and if you consciously listen, they'll deposit gems of insight to support your evolution and you'll return to your center of peace, power, passion, and pleasure that was always inside.

So if you're sad this Mother's Day, tell the truth and have a good cry. If you're angry, hit a pillow for ten minutes. If you're on top of the world, celebrate and dance! If you're feeling sexy, shine baby! Trust as you would trust the weather.

And the most important lesson to get your groove back is to be grateful for the lessons of single motherhood.

You, amazing woman, are:

Courageous, raising your child on your own
Honoring yourself, leaving what no longer worked
Industrious, figuring things out on your own without consistent help
Bold, as you learn to ask for help
Present, giving your attention to the kids versus being a victim because you don't see them all the time
Confident, holding your head high, seeing divorce as a learning experience versus feeling like a failure
Surrendered, healing your wounded heart and releasing grudges
Strong, opening your heart again to love, knowing that self-love makes you radiant

Now, to keep the sensual, vibrant juices flowing this Mother's Day and always, be sure to DANCE regularly to work through the weather patterns of feelings that may arise. Just one song is really all it takes. Right before you get going in the morning, right after you come home from dropping them off at school, right when you all get home as a celebratory releasing and grounding way to transition into family and home and joy.

Next, FORGIVE.

If you haven't already, forgive yourself.

You did your best and are doing your best. Remember to focus on what you've learned by the experience. Forgive him and be grateful that you're wiser and more self-assured. I like to write the statement "Thank you FORGIVing me the experience of divorce for now I've learned, now I know, now I understand, now it's clear, now it's time to..." This helps with integration so that we can move forward with power.

Finally, PLAY.

Set yourself free to enjoy a delicious, goofy, and joyful day with your kids, honoring the incredible woman you are. Not only does it encourage happy hormones to surge through your body, you're creating memories that strengthen your family while also practicing trust that the universe is on your side. You CAN let go and things won't fall apart. You CAN play and enjoy life to its fullest!

WHAT THIS MEANS FOR YOU...

Write a letter of appreciation to yourself for being a single mother.

Or if you're not, write a letter to yourself for all the times you've FELT like a single mother. Many married moms I know feel very alone, unappreciated, and disconnected from a powerful co-parenting relationship.

You see, when we're empty, it's challenging to find solutions.

But when we honor and acknowledge ourselves, not waiting for others to notice (and in so doing give our power away), from fullness we are more clear, creative, courageous and clever.

And between me, you and the fence post, you ROCK.

Part 5:
The Babe Gets That she's a Sacred Goddess...

We Never Get There So Go With the Flow

Who in the world has an ounce of creativity left when we're operating on fumes? I know I used to resort to putting on a video for my son just to give myself time to have a shower some mornings. Would you like to know how I turned things around, and how we would hit the Santa Monica Pier in costumes and have picnics in the driveway with the sun setting on our happy faces, playing the matching game?

I think a great caretaker of children, of our mates, of our careers, and of our sanity knows how to find balance moment to moment. Just like the journey is really the destination, balance is not to be found, only experienced in the moment. Same as love is never captured, only given and received moment to moment.

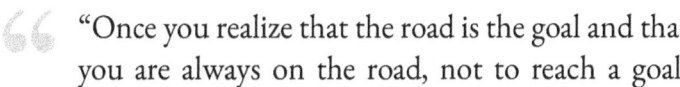

"Once you realize that the road is the goal and that you are always on the road, not to reach a goal, but to enjoy its beauty and its wisdom, life ceases to be a task and becomes natural and simple, in itself an ecstasy." —Sri Nisargadatta Maharaj

Given that there's no outcome of parenting really—a happy successful child I suppose—yet our job is never done. We just keep being presented with the moment to moment embrace of experiences. Then I don't have to do it perfectly!!! I just need to do my best and let the next evolution of my compassion, strength, patience, or playfulness be birthed. I will never be given something I can't handle, the Universe is always on my side, I have all I need in each moment to succeed, and so breathe, let go, and show up.

If discipline is called for, GREAT. And if silliness is called for, I can be silly, too. For me, being a great caretaker is being present to what my son needs, what I need, what WE need for this moment to be its best. Sometimes I need a time out, not him, ME! Sometimes the universe knows better than me, like recently when the author of Parenting Without Stress called ME after reading my weekly newsletter, seeing that I needed some support. Thank you, God!

I have wasted so much energy trying to control the moment. We have swim class to get to NOW.

We were planning on going to the chiropractor NOW. It's summer and he HAS to wear shorts.

It's July and we DON'T watch "Polar Express" until Christmas.

Just who is coming up with all these rules? Me.

And who is deciding to resist my son's enthusiasm for the moment? Yep, me again.

Of course there are structures, deadlines, rules, and propriety that I adhere to so that he can operate successfully in society, but would it kill him (or more honestly, kill me) if he wore his Superman costume to the grocery store with me? Would it kill me if we played catch for five minutes and THEN I made dinner? Would one more story really ruin my evening? Well sometimes I did have client calls and he needed to learn to respect my commitments, yet other times I was the one that just needed to chill.

Truly my most powerful learning and biggest gift to myself and my son is learning to let go, trust, surrender, listen for guidance, and take action with what inspires me, delights me, intrigues me. It's a lot of pressure being a parent, wanting to do your best, wanting their lives to be exceptional, learning to breathe as they experience their first letdowns.

One day as I was trying to get him to preschool NOW, he was down near the end of the driveway and I screamed, "SEAT! NOW!" Exasperated he screamed back, "Mom, I'm looking at the world!" That stopped me in my tracks. What was twenty to thirty seconds more to look at the sky, the birds, the house across the street, the cars, whatever he saw? Once I joined him, let him show me his world, we easily got in the car and I told him I didn't like to get angry and asked how could I be a better mom.

He told me, "Relax." Point taken.

And the real point taken is that I now have extra energy to be sexy, take care of me, and find creative things to do with him. When I'm not wasting my energy in fight or flight, draining my adrenals and making myself look ten years older than I am, wow, I feel amazing and I'm told I'm sexy! AND Gabe asks for more snuggles and listens better!

Yes, whenever we get "there," "here" we are again, so let's relax and enjoy the challenges and go with the flow in our families, in our careers, in our relationships, and in our minds.

Seventeen Sexy Mom-Time Solutions With Your Little Muffins!

Read these suggestions as joyful things to do with your children, your mate, your girlfriends. They're all meant to fill you up from the inside out to radiate your true sensual nature of savoring moments.

1. Play Guitars on the Front Porch

Why play inside when you can offer the neighborhood a concert? It really made us feel like we were a band. We'd open the door as if the curtain was rising and we'd be willing to look and sound silly but sing full out.

2. Dancing on the Coffee Table

Sure I had rules like no jumping on the bed so he wouldn't fall off and crack his head open, allowing that made no sense, I get it. Yet I had a super sturdy, huge coffee table that, that when one stood upon it, one can see perfectly into the mirror over the fireplace. So we'd rock out to kids' music or reggae songs like "One Love".

3. Bouncing on Ball in Exercise Room

One way I was able to get my workout in was to allow my son to climb up behind me on the big exercise ball, we'd hold hands, and bounce to his favorite songs. This really worked out my thighs and we pretended we were doing a concert like a cool rock band. Exercise was so important for our energy, confidence, and release of stress. Do whatever it takes to schedule it and be willing to be creative with the kids!

4. Wash the Truck and Water Fight

Who doesn't love a clean vehicle and a great water fight? Enlist the boyfriend or hubby because getting all wet's pretty sexy. Get the kids involved and let go of control as you let them get wet, wild, and feel wonderful.

5. The Tramp

I love the trampoline for being crazy and free and also bouncing and relaxing my tense body. I like to wear myself out and lay there under the huge sky with my little man or my boyfriend, suspended and floating above the Earth. Tramps are also GREAT for connecting with little boys who just won't sit still. Notice that you can really learn what's going on inside their mind and heart when you're simply bouncing and asking questions. Watch him open up.

6. Drawing on the Steps

Words carry energy, so we'd often write on our front steps in chalk, "Welcome to the house of love, joy, and strawberries" (my son helped with content). We'd also paint the cement in the back yard with washable paint and do affirmations. (One summer we pretended we were Cirque du Soleil dancers and painted our bodies, too.)

7. Grocery Store in Costume

What's the big deal really if Sunday morning you just let go of control and head to the grocery store in costumes with your kid's favorite stuffed animal? Doing things against the rules creates stunning memories for the family and many men say there's nothing sexier than a woman at peace in her skin. And in this case in her Swamp Queen outfit!

8. Fortress for Dinner

My son and I used to drape blankets over the big kitchen table, bring in our flash light, him dressed up as a super hero, and me in a crazy long wig and dress looking like a goddess, and we ate macaroni and cheese with our fingers by flashlight. Crazy? Yes. Fun? Totally. Sexy? Perhaps not as much as stripping for my partner in lingerie, yet most men find it very attractive when a woman is willing to be imaginative and playful. It DOES translate into the bedroom!

9. Dinnertime Make a Wish Ritual

Dinner time can often get rushed, be predictable, results-oriented (eat their veggies), and a stress for many moms to accomplish. The way I made it more rewarding and nourishing was to light candles every night. My son and I would light one for each other, his father, our friends and family. It created a calm mood for us to really connect and be present to each other. Then when we blew them out, we made wishes for ourselves and our friends and family. It just felt good. Try it.

10. Thank You's at Night

Most parents are great at nighttime rituals of books and songs, yet I would encourage you to also add gratitude to the list. My son and I did "thank you's" each night. Thank you for our health and wealth, family, and friends. Yet he remembered things I forgot like milk, stars, tickles, and angels. We'd also say thank you for challenges because they taught us lessons of patience, forgiveness, and tolerance. He even enlisted his dad to say them at his house.

11. "Polar Express" in June

Yes, I gave in, made hot chocolate, and got out the huge box the fake Christmas tree came in (which reminded my son of a train car), and we snuggled in with blankets and watched "Polar Express." He still remembers it.

12. Prayers and Candles at Dinner Table

Rituals really help you become present, sensually savoring moments. We lit candles every night at dinner. We had a rudimentary prayer of "Thank you for food, family, friends and fun." When we blew out the candles we made wishes for ourselves and then for others with the extra candles. This could be instantly spiced up if you're dining with your lover ... I wish that you'd tie me up.

13. The Matching Game for Dinner Time

I'm big on discipline and manners and yet I balanced it out with fun so we had regular picnics at sunset in the driveway with blankets, pillows, and his favorite matching card game. Sometimes people who walk by after dinner stop and help out. Hysterical, yet welcoming and community-building and fun!

14. Meditation Time Together

Remember when I said my son couldn't come into my room until seven zero zero? Well, one morning he broke the rule and I was meditating and I simply said he could join me or go back in his room. I couldn't believe it—he joined me. I was chanting Sanskrit and he loved it. Every so often after that he'd come in and want me to chant for him. How divine.

15. Reading and Ju Jitsu in Bed

Some mornings we'd have to get off to school, yet I loved the mornings when we could read together and then he'd attack me with his Ju Jitsu moves and we'd wrestle. I'm sure the teachers should thank me for getting his energy out first!

16. Thank You's and Song at Bedtime

I wanted to teach my son about gratitude—that what you focus on expands— and yet I also wanted to teach him to embrace even the challenges, learn the lessons, and let it all go versus holding onto grudges. So each night we'd say our "thank you's" and I'd help him to be grateful for everything the universe provided to expand and open us.

17. Painting ... Well, Everything!

Maybe this was just because I had a boy, but I remember my sister and I painting on paper, in the lines. Yet my son would rather paint his body and the ground, and why not? Get some washable paint, pretend you are Cirque du Soleil dancers, and then hop in the kiddy pool to wash off! Being "bad" sometimes gives you a lot of leeway building brownie points when you need to ask them to behave properly later.

Nine Things to Stop Doing to Live With Strength, Sensuality, and Soul

We've talked a lot about my journey, how to embrace challenges, how to stay in your body, how to fill yourself up. We've talked about energy, sensuality, communication, and taking care of yourself.

I want you to read the next section from the place of not bing only a woman, or only a mom, or only a career woman, or only a sister, daughter, wife or single, married or step mom. I want you to read it KNOWING, BELIEVING, AND ACCEPTING the fact that you are a gift to the planet, a divine expression of the divine feminine, that you are sacred and magical and powerful beyond measure.

Read these ways of being as a Queen High Priestess Royal Highness would read them. This is how I think. I have a kingdom (queendom) to run. Notice if it makes you sit taller, open your heart wider, become more grounded like a tree with roots deep into Mother Earth.

Notice when you begin implementing this way of BEING in your life, that your decisions change, that your kids start behaving more, that your partner asks if you've lost weight or did you get your hair cut. You will have begun radiating THE SACRED FEMININE ITSELF. You will be a vessel through which this energy fuels and nourishes and sustains your life. You are not alone nor do you have to do this all alone. You are supported. Yet you must believe and open to create the space for support. And it will come. In fact, it's already all around you.

The Sacred Feminine stops thinking from her head and thinks from her body, her heart, her pelvis, as if her pelvis was her brain, her intelligence, her wisdom.

When the kids have a tantrum, you ask your heart, "What would love do right now?"

The Sacred Feminine stops worrying about how she stacks up to the next woman and comes from overflowing abundance, which allows her to see her sister in every woman she meets.

When you're at the grocery store, you compliment a sister, "You look great!"

The Sacred Feminine stops holding her stomach and vagina tight thinking this will somehow keep her safe, and instead lets go of control by letting go physically in her shoulders, stomach, pelvis, and she feels the energy and the serendipity flow through and around her.

Honestly, this means talking through your other set of lips. (Yes, that's what I said.) Try sourcing your communications from the flow, from your feminine core and see what happens.

The Sacred Feminine stops being dramatic and having addictive intellectual stories about her emotions and processes. Instead she starts feeling in her body, expressing more sounds and less words to communicate her truth.

Simply try when the kids annoy you, delight you, when you partner pisses you off, turns you on... "mmmmm..." or "ouch..." or my favorite "hiss..."

The Sacred Feminine stops trying to control the world by being nice and getting people to like her by manipulating them or allowing them to manipulate her, and instead she simply breathes fully in and out and enjoys being with people in the moment, authentically curious about what might happen next.

At a playdate, no need to clench up and hope little Johnny doesn't whack little Sammy again. You just breathe, open, visualize the best, focus on the moment, and trust all is well and you are all surrounded by a cocoon of light and love.

The Sacred Feminine stops trying to understand, strategize,

and figure life out, which is pushing energy and stops all flow of creativity, intuition, and support from Mother Earth. Instead she opens, all luscious, juicy, and trusting as she surrenders to the fact that it's supposed to be a mystery.

Imagine opening the top of your head like a huge door, receptive to guidance while imagining your legs like roots into Mother Earth, your ally here to support and nourish you, and then simply move, dance, listen, flow, and trust what comes as the next step.

The Sacred Feminine stops competing with the universe thinking that she knows best. Instead she speaks her truth, making an intention and then surrenders to a connection that has always and will always be there, a connection that brings her dream or something even beyond her imagination and lays it gently at her feet.

All day long I like to say, "Something wonderful is happening today, and I look for it, expect it, know it's coming." Not attached to when, more a curious delight in the mysterious unfolding of it all.

The Sacred Feminine stops deflecting pleasure, joy, and success out of concern about what people will think and instead allows a love so deep, wide, and pure that she feels like her heart will explode. And then explodes into deeper and wider love and sees what life is like on the other side of fear.

When the kids show you their art, express what you REALLY feel! When the orgasm is building, let 'er rip! (I swear that little angels cover kids' ears so mommies can have really loud, expressive moans of pleasure.)

The Sacred Feminine stops trying to connect, trying to be good, trying to make a difference, trying to do the right thing, and knows that she need do nothing but BE to BE of value, to bring comfort to a child, to bring warmth to a lover, to bring tenderness to a friend, to bring light to this world.

Wake knowing you're done. You're enough. You're cooked. You're great. And from that fullness of already getting there, BE, give, enjoy, savor, love.

This is how I invite in the Sacred Feminine. I invite in an energy that unites with me for the highest good of all. I affirm that I am woman, sensuality itself, life itself, and I imagine my vagina lips opening and connecting to Mother Earth, sinking down and breathing in Mother Earth's energy, her power to create the Grand Canyon with a glance, the tenderness to blow a gentle breeze across of field of wheat in the prairies, the fierce love to protect her young from harm, the sultry, dark temptress energy to be ravished by a man of worth, the wise and unreasonable intuition to know to take an alternative route to work bypassing a deadly ten car pile-up. The Sacred Feminine is everything and oh, yes, she is sexy, yet from the inside. Because she is sensuality itself, sexuality itself, she knows she is sexy and need not prove it, just BE it and it is this knowing that is the number one turn- on for men.

The Sacred Feminine opens to everything. She's not afraid for she is fear itself. She's not addictively excited for she is joy itself. She's everything! The Sacred Feminine is overflowing and full from the inside out, thus she's not needy and can't be manipulated. The Sacred Feminine knows that she is capable of everything yet can improve efficiency and heighten her own creativity by delegating and asking for help so that her whole kingdom thrives. The Sacred Feminine knows that the more she fills herself up, the more she has to give to others. She is at peace in her skin, and sees other women as her sisters. She knows that feminine energy is more powerful than masculine energy, not better, just more powerful. A sailor is humbled by the power of the ocean to deliver him to a safe shore or kill him, and as wielders of this power, we must use it with honor, integrity, and truth.

Feminine energy can give birth and destroy life. To live in the Sacred Feminine is a great responsibility and yet well worth the journey. To access the Sacred Feminine's wisdom and power, a woman must live in her intuitive and feeling body. She must blend that embodied intelligence not with the spinning of her head, but the brilliance of her mind. She knows that movement, breath, and dancing is her ticket to pleasure, healing, truth, and power. The Sacred Feminine can't find her passion when operating on fumes. She doesn't wait for her marriage, health, or sanity to give before she take precious regular and nourishing ME time. The Sacred Feminine is our birthright... and she's inside you.

Glorious, amazing mother, take time each day, especially while walking or moving, to breathe her in through your feet, through your pelvis, and once full, up towards your heart. This is how I stay grounded, present, confident, radiant, and peaceful.

THE MOTHER

MY AWAKENING THROUGH A DIRECT EXPERIENCE AT AN ILLUMINATION INTENSIVE RETREAT

When I take the time to drop out of my head, Mother is waiting. She is beneath me and in me all at once. I access Her by exhaling into my vagina, opening up the lower part of my body, and sinking into the Earth. She is the Earth. It is as if I open the lips of my vagina and sink into her, deep down in the dark, delicious, messy power of Her. I let Her fill me with her energy, her love, her power. As I open and sink in, I also open my heart as if to unzip myself and be splayed open, inside out, heart vibrantly displayed for all to be nurtured from. In this open place, connected to Her as the Earth, I am indestructible, for I am all.

The Mother is everything. Every emotion lives in the Earth. This is where we give birth and where we can kill. This is where we are sultry and where we are innocent. This is where we are sensuality itself. Splayed open, sinking down, connected deep in Her, we aren't afraid for we are fear itself. We aren't excited because we are joy itself. From this place in the Mother as the Mother, we know everything for we are wisdom itself.

It is as if with a breath we can create a forest and with an exhale we can slice open a canyon. As we breathe, the fields of wheat sway back and forth. We are supported here by our sisters, sister goddesses. We hold each other, celebrate each other, honor each other all held in the womb of creation Herself.

The Mother energy is there to be tapped into at will. It takes courageous surrender to let go into her lap. Total and complete openness to the unknown is the key to open her doorway and to come home. Intend that she fill you and then let go in silence and stillness or in sacred dance.

When splayed open, filled to overflowing with Her love and energy, we no longer need anything, our vagina, heart, and world is filled to overflowing and we simply sway in the breeze of life itself. We no longer need outside influences of male companionship or career success to be filled. Instead we choose these for the sake of experience, to taste another flavor of life, to experience the unknown in union with another moment. The quality of man who dares step before a woman splayed open as love itself is a noble man indeed. She literally can't even see a man of less stature or questionable integrity when in this place and wouldn't even consider lowering her standards for she is life itself. It is only when a woman disconnects from the

Mother that she lives in the illusion of being filled from the outside.

When a woman filled to overflowing looks at her children, she has an infinitely wide range of responses to address their behavior, often accessing humor versus frustration, a knowing glance versus a draining yell. A women filled to overflowing with the Mother knows her worth—she is everything after all—so she doesn't try. She simply chooses how she'd like to bring light to the world and welcomes all serendipitous events into her life aligned with that direction. Total peace and knowing that her gifts are being given with each breath and not waiting for an external job offer to let her rest. She rests in her glory and wisdom and radiance already.

She is life itself. The Mother is us. We are everything already inside. The key to living as the Mother is dissolving your search out there, and resting, sinking, coming home on the inside, opening to your feminine core, the sacred womb, and letting Her fill you, letting Her guide you, letting Her be you in the world.

WHAT THIS MEANS FOR YOU...

JUST BE WITH THIS.

I wrote from a very primal, raw, deep place.

It may offend you, stir awakenings in you, completely resonate with you, make you uncomfortable.

Every reaction is perfect. Just BE with your response.

Don't try to change it.

I believe this energy that I've embraced, awakened, let have its way with me, is responsible for every good thing in my life.

Even the stuff that disappoints me, because I trust it's simply moving things out of the way for me to have an even grander expression of my truth revealed.

Permission to Have It All
(No Matter What All Looks Like)

YES PLEASE, I'LL HAVE A THRIVING MARRIAGE

I know, how am I, a twice-divorced, single mom, supposed to teach you anything about a thriving marriage? Well, we're here to teach what we're here to learn and I know what doesn't work which is the other half of what DOES work. The most important thing to me is creating a safe place for profound communication to occur. Without this, it's all fake, withheld, full of misunderstandings, not feeling heard, valued, or loved. It becomes a world of walking on eggshells.

YES, AND I'LL ALSO HAVE A FLOURISHING FAMILY, THANK YOU

I was raised in a dysfunctional family (but who wasn't?) and I felt strangely comfortable with chaos, pressure, and fighting. I wasn't always able to forgive the past and it was affecting my family's ability to flourish. I knew if it was going to get done, I'd have to do my inner work. Inner peace creates outer peace every time.

FABULOUS, I'LL TAKE A REWARDING CAREER, TOO PLEASE

I absolutely love my career. There is nothing in the whole wide world I'd rather be doing. I started working with my father in his pharmacy, being prepped to take over the store. The customers loved me, I did a good job, my dad was so proud, but I hated it. From it, I alchemized wisdom from the experience, learning that I loved people and decided to find a better fit in a new career. I decided to be a professional dancer. I had danced ballet, jazz, and tap as a child and I thought it would be fun to travel the world on cruise lines. Mom and Dad had a conniption. But I went for it anyway. I hopped on Uncle Phil's semi to be a dancer and ended up getting a gig in Tokyo which led to modeling, acting, being a spokesperson, and an interviewer. It's possible to follow your heart, know when to let go of something good and make room for great, incorporate the lessons from each stage, and keep expanding all the while not living for tomorrow but savoring today.

I'LL ABSOLUTELY BE A GREAT CARETAKER

While there's a tendency to put dead people on pedestals, yet I really did have an amazing mom. She made a point of doing all these cool things with us before we were five—the formative years. Go on a one-car ferry, go to a cattle auction (you can tell I'm from rural Canada), go to Vancouver and drink the water and taste how it's different from the water up in the mountains, and go to the island every spring break to hunt for crabs. This kind of thing, even finger paint in shaving cream on our old burnt orange 70's kitchen table. With me and my son, I admit to putting on a video just so I could squeeze in a shower some mornings. But I made peace with that.

OH, YEAH BABY, I AM MOST CERTAINLY A SMOKIN' HOT MAMA

You know how truly sexy women don't even know their sexy? And how the rest of us TRYING to be sexy aren't so sexy? A smokin' hot mama is in my opinion a mama who is so in love with her self, not narcissistically, but authentically, that she need not get approval from the outside, she doesn't get her gratification from having her kids show up perfectly or her husband say the exact right thing. She isn't controlling, seeking, driven to accomplish to be enough. She is completely at peace in her skin and takes loving actions towards her higher expression of happiness. She naturally exercises, eats well, says "no" when she means "no" and "yes" when she means "yes," and enjoys her form of fashion expression and simply loves being a woman.

AND YES, I'M READY TO TRULY SEE MYSELF AS A DIVINE GODDESS

There is a place I go when I dance. I swear, Spirit dances me. Some other energy is moving my hips, I feel connected to the earth so much that it's as if I'm making love to the earth with my feet versus the clenched permanent kegel I used to walk around with. There is a place I go when I breathe deeply that makes my voice lower, my anxiety dissolve, and my eyes slightly soften—like they look after I orgasm, all lashes. There is a way I look at my son as the sunset streams through his hair that moves me to tears. There is a way that I can sit with my girlfriends on the couch and laugh, and cry and hold each other like sisters and not have to fix a thing and just open wide to the tragedies and triumphs of life. If this kind of living draws you, pulls you from a deep place in your heart, read my article and learn the many ways you can live your birthright today.

Conclusion: Inspiring You To Live Lusciously From the Inside Out

My inspiration for this book stems from my belief and firsthand experience that **When Mama's Happy, Everybody's Happy.** Period.

I want moms to understand, learn, and practice regular self-care so that they know their natural state is being a beautiful and sensual woman who is a patient mom, ravishing lover, heartfelt girlfriend, and happy with exactly who she is from the inside out. I want to guide moms to let go of the babe they were, embrace the babe they are, and fill their tanks so full that not only will they always be a babe—sexy, sensual, and satisfied —they will always have a store of energy, patience, and self-worth for when life presents challenges and change. Being sexy from the inside out is a shift in perspective from outside attention to inside self-approval. When we love and care for ourselves fully, our lives no longer become about getting attention, doing it right, or looking good. Our lives become about enjoying the process and empowering our marriage, inspiring our family and community. It becomes about celebrating the journey and living our purpose creatively. To me, this is the true meaning of power, joy, and inner peace.

YOU, a luscious goddess who knows she's not only the divine mother yet also the Sacred Feminine herself, must regularly practice ...

Listening to yourself: What do you need? Give it to yourself.

Find your groove as a mom: Kids don't have handbooks.

Be patient as you figure yours out.

Getting your body back: It took nine months to get here so be patient and find a routine that makes you feel empowered and delicious!

Decide your career path: Back to work or a stay-at-home mom? Both are great choices. Make the choice that's YOUR truth, not society's expectations.

Have sex again: As you learn to love your body as it is today, so will he. As within, so without.

Motherhood is a time of letting go...

> Of control: You can't control this little munchkin, let alone the universe, so relax and enjoy the crisis and find the humor whenever possible.
> Of suffering: Have a really good cry, hit some pillows, and release what's stuck inside. Then begin to ask for help and get the support you need.
> Of competition: With others or with your old self, know you are always doing your best and that's enough. You rock, okay?
> Of trying to change the present: What you resist persists, so surrender and find peace with what it is and watch everything become smoother and begin falling aside or into place.

Motherhood is excellent practice for reaching out...

To other moms who can relate: Time to create the moms group (not a gossip, man-bashing group, although authentic expression and honesty is a must).
To helpers: Before you snap, hire a sitter, nanny, ask a friend or family member for a few hours each week for YOU. Feel the guilt and do it anyway. Guilt is a manufactured emotion anyway, so stop letting it sabotage your self-care.
To him: Express your gratitude for him. Ask for regular US time and ALONE time and ask for being held, a foot massage, a reminder why he chose you. Create dreams and a future to live into together.
To fashion: Banish sweats and adorn thyself! Try a moms clothes swap, a trip to the mall, or an image consultant. Looking good makes you feel good. I'm serious, do it!
To the Goddess within you: Your sexiness is a full expression of pure love of self, pure feminine divinity, pure goddess. She's in there—find her, express her, enjoy being her.

Be a sexy Mom, a luscious MILF, a yummy mummy... practice these eleven keys for your own fulfillment and for his.

1. Reconnect with Your Body

Dance regularly in honor of your body. Let go of the world on your shoulders, let go of fears and anger, turn yourself on by how great it feels to be a woman. Be filled with inspiration, energy, and light and give that to yourself, your relationship, and family.

2. Reconnect with Him

Be yourself and dance for him! Your body is an amazing miracle that created life! Shine, grind, and undulate as a vessel of light no matter what your size. The more you love you, he will too.

3. Speak Your Truth

Face your fears and tell the truth. When you're honest, it's easier to be kind and real. Withholding or settling leads to whiny victims, resignation, and depression in no time.

4. Celebrate the Mundane

Attitudes and thoughts are our choice. If you don't resist the diapers and laundry, you'll have more energy to savor moments like a foot rub or date night. Everyone will notice your shift. Then watch them join you!

5. Take Time to Listen Deeply

Do you know what you yearn for? What you need to let go of? Do you really stop to listen to his answer to "how was your day?" Teach your kids about listening and "mommy time" and they will learn to listen and honor their own space as they grow.

6. Breathe "Yes" and Be Open

To whatever comes each day ... There's a lesson in everything and you can teach your kids to trust in themselves because they watch a mom who can handle whatever comes her way with a deep breath, which in my opinion is a breathe of grace.

7. Say Thank You's
Each night at dinner or bedtime, be grateful, even for the tough stuff, and let go of the day, let go of the past, and make room for a new day and new opportunities to grace your path.

8. Have a Good Sob
Be gentle with yourself even when you're not a picture-perfect mom and let off steam. Self-love is really the acceptance of all aspects of self, even our shadow selves, and a bath and a sob is cleansing and calming.

9. Dress as a Sexy Woman Even if You Don't Feel Like It
We do not see things as they are, we see things as WE are, so see yourself as a sexy women adored by a benevolent universe, and it shall be so.

10. Keep Your Girlfriends Close
Nothing replaces girl time. They take your temperature and warn you when you're not your usual glow. Celebrate the journey with them and be generous with them, too. They're the glue of your life.

11. Laugh Often
Whether you need to stage a tickle fight with Dad to get the juices flowing or jump in the bounce castle with the kids,

taking life a little less seriously will raise the bar on your sex appeal. Sexy is a confident woman who can laugh at herself.

MOTHERHOOD IS ABOUT FACING AND EMBRACING CHANGE AND CHALLENGES

Keeping your Marriage Thriving and Alive Through the Ebbs and Flows: It's a plant. It needs watering, occasional weeding, regular sunshine, some fabulous fertilizer. You'll know what element is in need, trust yourself, and enjoy the harvest.

Divorce: You didn't fail, you more deeply committed to you. Be sure to do everything you can to be sure you've given it everything you've got before you end it, unless of course you're in danger. This way you'll be able to bless and release him and move on wiser, more empowered, and clear with what partnership you need that's in your highest good and the highest good of all.

Ex's & Being the Step-mom: It is what it is. What can you change about YOU? Perspective! Ask "Why is this perfect? What's the opportunity here? Why is this the best way to birth something in me? What does this provide that's only possible this way?" Growth doesn't always come in pretty packages, yet it builds strength, compassion, resiliency, and courage. And you might even come to be grateful for what is.

Widowhood: When the unthinkable happens, it's important to have support in going from heartbreak to happiness. I recommend my friend, colleague, and coach Aurora Winter at And know you are loved.

Parenting: Give yourself a break and be open to learning some parenting skills. You're not a bad person, there's just no manual! Learn how positive discipline, mutual respect, and non-violent communication can make tantrums dissolve and peace unfold.

Here's what helped me.
Right Brain Child in a Left Brain World by J. Freed
Non-violent Communication by M. Rosenberg

And so my amazing, beautiful mothers, who may be new moms or empty nesters, know that you are doing a magnificent job, know that you are validated for all you feel, know that you are understood and heard, completely gotten for all that's churning inside you.

Know you are more than beautiful, you are beauty itself, that your sensuality is your access to power, patience, playfulness, and your purpose ... it fuels you, your marriage, and your family. Slow down and truly feel my love envelope you like a soft warm blanket. Allow yourself to exhale all the way out, to rest, to let go, to be.

Know your children are sooooo blessed to have you, that you are an amazing mother, and the more you implement these practices and perspectives into your life, you will enjoy motherhood more and the kids will benefit beyond words. And your man will stand in awe of the goddess he's married, or your radiance will attract the man who will cherish you. Regardless, you will feel full, juicy, grateful, and vibrantly alive being exactly who you are, and humbled that you GET to be a mother. Thank you for the gift that you are to so many. You're always in my heart. I love you and believe in you.

Deliciously yours, still dancing through the mystery of life,
Allana

P.S. Below are some delicious messages from me that you can print out and place in your diaper bag, your glove compartment, your makeup drawer, your laundry room ... in places where you may just need a little reminder from time to time that you're a rockin' divaluscious, amazing mama.

P.P.S. I looooooove you!

Just a reminder to stop. Breathe. Open. Allow life to press itself into you and hold you. Rest.

Trust, slow down, and feel life weaving its magical tapestry around you, through you, as you.

Are you celebrating your life in this moment?
Find something to celebrate about exactly where you are and give a little hoot and holler. Louder. That's better.

Have I told you today that you're beautiful?
Yup. You're shining so bright I can feel you all the way from here. And all you had to do was be YOU.

What if being exactly who you are is enough?
Because I think you're delicious ...

You are from Mother Nature,
and thus like all her creations, perfect.

You are ageless, not because of a face-lift, but because you've simply stopped resisting your age.

Are you loving your kids who are away from you in this moment? I know it's damn hard not to worry,
but it drains you, so stretch your heart open and surround them in a cocoon of love right this minute!

Wear that special occasion sexy lingerie TODAY.
It'll be our little secret.

I know it's dorky, but right now stop and give yourself
a hug. (People will think you're stretching.)
You're doing such a great job.

Do something you've been putting off... yes, that.
Even just the first step. I believe in you.

Relax your brow, your face, your scalp, your shoulders.
You're enough whether or not this all gets done.

Are you accepting of your body in this moment?
Find a part to love and smother it
with your delicious compliments.

Resources for You and Your Man

DIRECT FROM ME TO YOU
<u>*FOR YOU GORGEOUS:*</u>

How to Be and Stay Sexy, Ebook and Audio

https://allanapratt.com/product/how-to-be-and-stay-sexy/

Thriving Intimacy for Her, 35 Days of Guided Meditations

https://allanapratt.com/product/thriving-intimacy-guided-meditations/

Sacred Erotic You

https://allanapratt.com/product/embracing-the-sacred-erotic-you/

HeartMates for Her

https://allanapratt.com/heartmates-for-her

Intimacy Blindspot Complimentary Quiz

https://allanapratt.com/quiz

Vulnerability (Free Training)

https://allanapratt.com/vulnerability

Allana Pratt
INTIMACY EXPERT

FOR YOUR MAN:

***Scoring a Relationship*, Ebook and Audio**

https://allanapratt.com/product/scoring-a-relationship/

***How to Be a Noble Badass*, Ebook**

https://allanapratt.com/product/how-to-be-a-noble-badass/

Thriving Intimacy for Him, 35 Days of Guided Meditations

https://allanapratt.com/product/thriving-intimacy-guided-meditations-for-him/

HeartMates for Him

https://allanapratt.com/heartmates-for-him

Intimacy Blindspot Complimentary Quiz

https://allanapratt.com/quiz

FOR BOTH OF YOU:

HeartMates for Us

https://allanapratt.com/heartmates-for-us

Intimacy Blindspot Complimentary Quiz

https://allanapratt.com/quiz

Allana Pratt
INTIMACY EXPERT

About Allana Pratt

Intimacy Expert, Allana Pratt is a global media personality and go-to authority for those ready to heal heartbreak, live unapologetically and attract a soul-shaking relationship. This Ivy League grad is the Author of 6 books, has interviewed Whoopi Goldberg and Alanis Morissette, and Hosts the edgy Podcast *Intimate Conversations: Season 11- Soul Medicine*, where listeners learn how to 'Become the One' to 'Find the One' which 'Keeps the One.'

A Certified Master Coach with close to 5 million viewers on YouTube, Allana was asked by Leeza Gibbons to coach her during *Dancing with the Stars*. Interviewed over 800 times, she's been chosen as an Icon of Influence and featured on Huffington Post, People Magazine, Forbes, CBS, ABC, FOX, TLC, iHeartRadio, the GoodMenProject and more.

For the past 20 yrs, Allana's brave willingness to heal her own heart and come Home to herself makes her authentic, relatable and credible in her proven Coaching Programs and Intimacy Retreats. Her wisdom, exuberance and raw transparency inspire the deep soul work required to create a solid intimate relationship with one's self first, which naturally attracts and enhances an ideal open-hearted partnership that lasts. She's a small town Canadian girl living in rural Wyoming who is honored to love the sh** out of Humanity.

- amazon.com/stores/author/B0086PTM46
- instagram.com/allanapratt
- twitter.com/allanapratt
- facebook.com/coachallanapratt
- youtube.com/allanapratt
- linkedin.com/in/allana-pratt-36b5882
- tiktok.com/@coachallanapratt

Also by Allana Pratt

Available on Amazon, in Paperback and eBook

From Heartbreak to Heartmates

How to Be and Stay Sexy

Finding 'the One' is Bullshit,
Becoming 'the One' is Brilliant & Beautiful

How to Be a Noble Badass

Scoring a Relationship

www.ingramcontent.com/pod-product-compliance
Lightning Source LLC
Chambersburg PA
CBHW022111090426
42743CB00008B/800